LEVITICUS
—and—
NUMBERS

Text copyright © Mike Butterworth 2003

The author asserts the moral right to be
identified as the author of this work

Published by
The Bible Reading Fellowship
First Floor, Elsfield Hall
15–17 Elsfield Way, Oxford OX2 8FG

ISBN 1 84101 192 4
10 9 8 7 6 5 4 3 2 1 0

Acknowledgments
Unless otherwise stated, scripture quotations are taken from
The New Revised Standard Version of the Bible, Anglicized Edition, copyright
© 1989, 1995 by the Division of Christian Education of the National Council
of the Churches of Christ in the USA, and are used by permission. All rights
reserved.

Scriptyure quotations from The Revised Standard Version of the Bible, copyright
© 1946, 1952, 1971 by the Division of Christian Education of the National
Council of the Churches of Christ in the United States of America are used by
permission All rights reserved.

Scripture quotations from the Holy Bible, New International Version, copyright
© 1973, 1978, 1984 by International Bible Society. Used by permission of
Hodder & Stoughton Ltd. All rights reserved. 'NIV' is a registered trademark of
International Bible Society. UK trademark number 1448790.

Extracts from the Authorized Version of the Bible (The King James Bible), the
rights in which are vested in the Crown, are reproduced by permission of the
Crown's Patentee, Cambridge University Press.

Extracts from The Book of Common Prayer of 1662, the rights of which are
vested in the Crown in perpetuity within the United Kingdom, are reproduced
by permission of Cambridge University Press, Her Majesty's Printers.

p. 159: Song extract by Graham Kendrick, copyright © Make Way Music,
PO Box 263, Croydon, Surrey, CR9 5AP, UK. Used by permission.

A catalogue record for this book is available from the British Library

Printed and bound in Great Britain
by Bookmarque, Croydon

LEVITICUS
—and—
NUMBERS

THE PEOPLE'S
BIBLE COMMENTARY

MIKE
BUTTERWORTH

A BIBLE COMMENTARY FOR EVERY DAY

Introducing the People's Bible Commentary
Series

Congratulations! You are embarking on a voyage of discovery—or rediscovery. You may feel you know the Bible very well; you may never have turned its pages before. You may be looking for a fresh way of approaching daily Bible study; you may be searching for useful insights to share in a study group or from a pulpit.

The People's Bible Commentary (PBC) series is designed for all those who want to study the scriptures in a way that will warm the heart as well as instructing the mind. To help you, the series distils the best of scholarly insights into the straightforward language and devotional emphasis of Bible reading notes. Explanation of background material, and discussion of the original Greek and Hebrew, will always aim to be brief.

- If you have never really studied the Bible before, the series offers a serious yet accessible way in.

- If you help to lead a church study group, or are otherwise involved in regular preaching and teaching, you can find invaluable 'snapshots' of a Bible passage through the PBC approach.

- If you are a church worker or minister, burned out on the Bible, this series could help you recover the wonder of scripture.

Using a People's Bible Commentary

The series is designed for use alongside any version of the Bible. You may have your own favourite translation, but you might like to consider trying a different one in order to gain fresh perspectives on familiar passages.

Many Bible translations come in a range of editions, including study and reference editions that have concordances, various kinds of special index, maps and marginal notes. These can all prove helpful in studying the relevant passage. The Notes section at the back of each PBC volume provides space for you to write personal reflections, points to follow up, questions and comments.

Each People's Bible Commentary can be used on a daily basis, instead of Bible reading notes. Alternatively, it can be read straight through, or used as a resource book for insight into particular verses of the biblical book.

If you have enjoyed using this commentary and would like to progress further in Bible study, you will find details of other volumes in the series listed at the back, together with information about a special offer from BRF.

While it is important to deepen understanding of a given passage, this series always aims to engage both heart and mind in the study of the Bible. The scriptures point to our Lord himself and our task is to use them to build our relationship with him. When we read, let us do so prayerfully, slowly, reverently, expecting him to speak to our hearts.

CONTENTS

PBC Leviticus & Numbers:
Introduction

Why read them today—and how?

It is important to read these two books in their context—or rather contexts. First of all, we remind ourselves that they are very ancient books with material in them going back into the second millennium BC, that is, before 1000BC. The actual date of composition is disputed by scholars (see below) but for our purposes this will not matter very much. What is important is to beware of reading our own modern ideas into the book, or imagining life in these ancient times as roughly similar to our own.

We also need to bear in mind the fact that Leviticus and Numbers are an integral part of the Pentateuch (Genesis to Deuteronomy) and that the storyline goes through these books and into Joshua, Judges, Samuel and Kings. The books Joshua to Kings are often referred to as the Deuteronomic (or Deuteronomistic) History, because the editor(s) of these books shows great affinities of thought and language with the book of Deuteronomy. Both, for example, put great emphasis on *remembering* what God has done, and on the need to avoid contamination by Canaanite practices. Both have an enthusiastic, exhortatory tone, and use similar characteristic words and phrases. Leviticus and Numbers take us to the edge of the promised land and prepare us for the fulfilment of the second great promise to Abraham. This promise or covenant first appears in Genesis 12:1–3, where Abraham is promised many descendants (already fulfilled by the end of the book of Genesis), blessing (relationship with God), a land, and to be a blessing to all nations. These promises are repeated time and time again throughout the Pentateuch and it is essential to realize this if we are to understand any part of it. This motif forms an overarching theme stretching from Genesis 12 to Joshua and beyond.

Contents of the Pentateuch

Book or section	Place of action	Main contents
Genesis 1—11	The whole universe	Creation of the world. Origin and spread of sin.
Genesis 12—50	Mesopotamia to Canaan ... to Egypt	Call of Abraham. Covenant continues through descendants. Promise of descendants partially fulfilled.
Exodus	Egypt to Sinai (via the Reed Sea)	Oppression in Egypt. Call of Moses. Liberation. Giving of the Law at Mt Sinai.
Leviticus	Mount Sinai	Priestly laws (with a few incidents). Stress on holiness. Focus on relationship with God.
Numbers	Sinai to borders of Canaan	Laws and statistics. Several rebellions. Focus moves towards the promised land.
Deuteronomy	Border of Canaan, east of the River Jordan	Moses' farewell address. Promise of land about to be fulfilled.

The contents of Leviticus and Numbers look quite forbidding (see below). But behind that stern exterior there are some very interesting and significant details, for these chapters provide essential background for understanding the New Testament, especially the sacrifice of Jesus Christ who 'died for our sins in accordance with the Scriptures' (1 Corinthians 15:3). They also raise crucial questions about the nature of God and fill out emphases that are present in the New Testament but are easily overlooked.

In the book of Leviticus, the following units are often identified: sacrificial rituals (chs. 1—7); laws concerning purity in public worship (chs. 11—15); Day of atonement (*Yom Kippur*) (ch. 16); holiness code (chs. 17—26); and vows (ch. 27). They are 'priestly' in nature —the sort of things that lay people would not need to know in detail but would experience as participants. There is very little straight narrative. In Numbers, on the other hand, we find a mixture of narrative plus technical material, this time mostly in the form of laws and statistics. The latter parts are roughly: statistics and laws, covering topics like jealousy, Nazirites, the dedication of the altar, Levites, the Passover, uncleanness, and sounding trumpets (chs. 1—10); laws about offerings (ch. 15); Aaron (ch. 18); the red heifer (ch. 19); miscellaneous matters including another census, the daughters of Zelophehad, offerings at feasts, vows, boundaries and divisions, and Levitical cities.

Overall, therefore, the Pentateuch tells the story of the beginnings of the nation of Israel. It gives us certain important foundations for the faith of Israel (and therefore our own faith): creation (God the Creator); sin; and God's way of dealing with it through covenant (grace). It might be regarded overall as the promise in writing to Abraham and his descendants. Other important themes are associated with these foundations, such as elaboration of the nature of God. This is conveyed by both *word*, including revelation of his Name and teaching about how to please him (law), and *action*, especially in delivering his people from slavery in Egypt by signs and wonders, and in sustaining and disciplining them on their journey to the promised land.

Scholarly work on the Pentateuch

For about 100 years, the study of the Pentateuch was dominated by the 'documentary hypothesis'. In its basic form, worked out in detail by Wellhausen, it said that the Pentateuch was composed from four continuous 'documents':

J **Jahwist (Yahwist):** It originated in Judah—that is, the southern kingdom—in about the 10th century BC. This source is happy to use the divine name 'Yahweh' (wrongly transcribed as 'Jehovah') right from the beginning of Genesis.

E **Elohist**, that is, the one who uses the word 'elohim' for God: This source does not use the name 'Yahweh' until Exodus 3. It originated in Ephraim—that is, the northern kingdom of Israel—in the 9th century.

D Deuteronomist: 7th century BC onwards; originated in the northern kingdom.

P Priestly writer: 5th century BC; originated in Judah after the exile. This source does not use the name 'Yahweh' until Exodus 6.

The theory is that these documents, which were originally independent units telling the story of Israel's beginning, were combined by editors at different stages in Israel's history. The theory was developed by German scholars in the 19th century, notably Graf, Kuenen and (especially) Wellhausen. You will often see, in scholarly or semi-scholarly books, the letter J, E, D or P placed after a reference to verses in the Pentateuch. Conservative Christians have usually regarded this negatively, since it was associated with a negative view of the historicity and accuracy of the Bible. After all, if something was only written down 200 to 700 years after the events described, one might well assume that it is not likely to be reliable. More recently, conservative scholars have been open to acknowledge the analysis into the sources J, (possibly E), D and P, without necessarily accepting the dating that goes with them.

In the last few years, however, there have been challenges to this theory from quite unconservative directions. J. Van Seters has argued, for example, that D was the earliest source, and was supplemented by J (indicating a wider source than that assumed by Wellhausen and others) and finally P. E did not exist as a document and the only continuous source was D. It is clear that we cannot enter into this sort of debate and, in any case, Van Seters has much greater confidence in his own arguments and significance than I do!

One of the most important developments since Wellhausen was that of form criticism. Hermann Gunkel, the originator of this branch of study, wanted to investigate the pre-literary stages of the text. In other words, was it possible to detect signs of the units that must have been (he assumed) passed on by word of mouth before the material was written down?

He looked at the *forms* of the material that we find in the Old Testament rather than the content. For example, 1 Kings 21:19, 'Thus says the Lord...', would be analysed as an *introductory (prophetic) formula* followed by a message in two parts: *accusation* and *threat*. Gunkel hoped to be able to specify the *setting in life* of these units of material, and so to build up a history of the composition of the text. In other words, he wanted to be able to describe the situation in which prophetic utterances were made. The passage in 1 Kings 21 gives us some information: the prophet goes to the place where the recipient of his message is to be found (that is, in the late Naboth's vineyard) and speaks in the name of God, using an introductory formula ('Thus says the Lord'—twice in this passage) and then direct speech of God. (In many passages, the prophet speaks in the first person singular, as if God were actually speaking.)

Gunkel's hope was that *forms* could be linked with actual *situations*. Compare our use of the form 'Dear Albert', which we would assume indicates a letter sent to someone to read for himself—and not, of course, read out loud to Albert personally in a vineyard or anywhere else. If we can do this successfully, then we can build up a picture of how spoken forms were gathered together and edited into a book—that is, put into written form.

Form criticism leads naturally, therefore, into two other related and overlapping activities:

1. 'Redaction criticism', which roughly means 'editing investigation' or enquiry into the work of the editors or redactors who put together the biblical text.

2. 'History of traditions' or 'traditio-historical criticism', which means tracing how the various traditions were altered and developed, combined and recombined, throughout Israel's history.

It seems to me that there is not enough evidence in the Old Testament to carry this through, and sure results are hard to come by. Scholars associated with this approach are G. von Rad (1938), A. Alt, M. Noth (1948), G. Fohrer (1964–65), R. Rendtorff (1977), and his pupil E. Blum (1984).

The form-critical approach led to a concentration on 'traditions' rather than 'documents'. Von Rad assigned an important place to both. Noth spoke mostly of 'traditions'. Scandinavian scholars concentrate on traditions. Rendtorff argued that the present large units of the Pentateuch developed independently and were combined only at a late stage (compare Van Seters, mentioned above).

In the late 1970s there was a surge of interest in literary readings of the Bible. Scholars began to say that there was justification for studying the received text, so that, whatever the date of the final version of the biblical books, we can study the finished product as something having its own integrity. This means that we do not have to try to get back to the 'original words' of the prophet (or whoever) and discard the rest as due to an editor or 'redactor' (to be said in a scornful voice). It means that if there were editors or redactors involved, then they had an important part to play in giving shape to the text. Not all scholars have been sympathetic to this approach.

The scholar who gave the biggest boost to this type of approach was B.S. Childs, whose *Introduction to the Old Testament as Scripture* (SCM Press, 1979) stimulated great interest and thought and changed the way many scholars approached Old Testament study. Childs took critical study seriously, but concentrated on the 'canonical form' of the text. He suggested that the editors provided important theological insight as they selected particular sources, added notes, probably deleted certain passages, and arranged the text so as to bring out particular emphases. This approach means that we assume that there is a theological purpose implied by the content and arrangement of the text of each book or major section of the Old Testament—Childs often uses the term 'canonical shaping'—and we try to discern what it is. I am not sure who these super theologians were but, if we have a modest belief in the providence of God, it does seem helpful to assume that this attempt at discernment is worthwhile and significant.

This conviction has inspired much work on 'rhetorical criticism', the study of how a text conveys its main teaching, its emphasis and its nuances. One element in this field of study would be the study of repetitions. In traditional source criticism, a repetition (of a word, phrase or whole narrative) was assumed to indicate two original sources. In rhetorical criticism, the question asked is, 'What might be the writer's purpose in presenting—or not removing—this repetition?' Rhetorical criticism has also produced many studies on the structure of passages in the Bible, including my own *Structure and the Book of Zechariah* (Sheffield Academic Press, 1992).

It is often difficult to believe that the biblical writer had in mind the sort of elegant and complicated structures that are 'discovered' in the text. In current scholarly writing, however, there are many who would be untroubled by this fact, since they operate within what is often called 'reader-response criticism'. It consists of focusing upon the reader, rather than on the text, and is often wedded to the conviction that we cannot and should not *try to discover the intention of the writer*. What matters is *what the reader makes of the text*. So we find books and articles that speak of 'a feminist reading of [for example] Genesis 1—3' or even a 'vegetarian' reading. This approach is the same in principle as some liberation theology, where it might be asserted that, for example, Exodus speaks directly to people who suffer from oppression, powerlessness, marginalization and so on. There are important insights within this view, in my opinion. For example, different readers see different things in a text and the intended readership or audience might give a helpful indication of the intention of the writer of speaker. Moreover, it is important to realize that we ourselves read the text from within a particular cultural situation, and that will affect our understanding of the text. We cannot read from a 'neutral, objective' position. This does not mean, however, that we are completely unable to discern what someone from a different age and culture is trying to say. Fathers sometimes even understand their teenage children—roughly speaking.

What are we to say, in view of the uncertain state of scholarly theories today? The most popular answer has been 'concentrate on the teaching of the text as we now have it'. This has been developed in different ways, but it would seem to be the most fruitful approach. It means that people with differing views of the authority of the Old Testament can agree on what they are studying. It means that the object of study, the Old Testament, is there before us: we do not have to separate 'authentic material' out from a mass of editorial additions. It means that we can concentrate on 'what the text says'. This is the approach of this particular commentary. I understand the text as communicating something to us rather than ourselves as 'making something of the text'. In discovering (not constructing) what that is, we shall be helped by investigating the background, finding out what words and concepts meant in ancient Israel, understanding history and social customs, and so on. We shall almost certainly get a lot of it wrong but we shall, I think, find that we enter into the world of the text and find hidden treasures.

The message of Leviticus and Numbers

The best way to grasp the theological teaching of these books is to read them, but here is a sort of checklist and 'what to look for' guide.

As a part of the greater narrative of the Pentateuch, Leviticus and Numbers have much in common. They assume that God is powerful: he redeemed his people from Egypt, he sustained and led them in the desert, providing food and water, he judged them when they disobeyed him. Hence he is not only powerful but holy, demanding obedience and respect in approaching him. Genesis 12:1–3 introduces God's covenant with Abraham, promising many descendants (fulfilled by the end of the book of Genesis), land, blessing to Abraham and his descendants (their relationship with the Lord is especially in focus), leading eventually to blessing for all families of the earth. Roughly speaking, it is 'relationship' that is in focus in Leviticus, while Numbers looks forward to inheriting the promised land.

Leviticus: holiness and well-being

The theme of God's holiness is especially emphasized in Leviticus. Chapters 16—26 repeat over and over again, 'I am holy'. Because God is holy, his people are required to be holy. The sacrificial regulations hammer home the message that all approaches to God must be on his terms. Laws about clean and unclean food provide physical illustrations of a spiritual requirement. The annual Day of Atonement provided a powerful multi-media visual aid towards appreciating the incompatibility of sin and the Lord. The fearful events of Leviticus 10 bring home the lesson with penetrating clarity.

At the same time, the ultimate purpose of all these regulations, these events and this teaching is the well-being of the people. God's aim stated in Genesis 17:8, and repeated at a key point in Israel's history in Exodus 6:7, is confirmed in Leviticus 26:12: 'I will walk among you, and will be your God, and you shall be my people.' All the judgments, however strict they may be, look towards the achievement of this goal, the holy God in fellowship with his holy people.

Numbers: God's patience and promise

Numbers contains all these themes, with an additional emphasis on the long-suffering nature of God. Its main focus is on the fulfilment of the promise of land. The people are ready to begin the conquest of Canaan in chapter 13, but they lose their nerve in the face of the pessimistic report of the spies, and refuse to believe God's promises. Despite this and several other rebellions, individual and corporate, God persists with the people and brings them to the borders of

Canaan. We shall meet some shocking examples of judgment, which we must wrestle with, and even God's most important servants, Miriam, Aaron and even Moses, are included. The theological message is clear. God's purpose was the same then as it was later, when he sent John the Baptist to prepare the way of the Lord, Jesus the Messiah, and the fulfilment of Israel's hopes.

Thus he has shown the mercy promised to our ancestors,
  and has remembered his holy covenant,
the oath that he swore to our ancestor Abraham,
  to grant us that we, being rescued from the hands of our enemies,
might serve him without fear, in holiness and righteousness
  before him all our days.
And you, child, will be called the prophet of the Most High;
  for you will go before the Lord to prepare his ways,
to give knowledge of salvation to his people
  by the forgiveness of their sins.
By the tender mercy of our God,
  the dawn from on high will break upon us,
to give light to those who sit in darkness and in the shadow of death,
  to guide our feet into the way of peace.

Luke 1:72–79

Technical terms

There are some technical terms in Hebrew for various sacrifices which are translated with different English phrases in different Bible translations. My preferred term, where relevant, is in bold type

References	NRSV	RSV	NIV	Other alternatives
Lev. 1 burnt offering	burnt offering	**burnt offering**		whole (burnt) offering
Lev. 2 cereal offering	grain offering	**cereal offering**	grain offering	
Lev. 3 peace offering	sacrifice of well-being	**peace offering**	fellowship offering	offering of well-being shared offering completion offering communion offering
peace offering might be offered as: (Lev. 7:12–16)	**thank offering** **votive offering** **freewill offering**	thank offering votive offering freewill offering	thank-offering result of a vow freewill offering	praise offering
Note also the following two related Hebrew terms, referring to peace offerings and translated in various ways.				
tenupha Ex. 29:27f.; Lev. 7:30; 9:21	elevation offering	**wave offering**	wave offering	AV wave offering WBC = NRSV

teruma Lev. 7:14, 32, 34; Num. 15:19–21; 18:8–29; 31:29, 31; Deut. 12:6, 11, 17,	offering [inc. Ex. 29:28], gift, donation, also translated 'elevation offering' in Exodus 29:27	**offering**	contribution; [thing] presented offering	AV, ASV heave offering WBC
Lev. 4:1—5:13 sin offering	**sin offering**	sin offering	sin offering	purification offering
Lev. 5:14—6:7 guilt offering	**guilt offering**	guilt offering	guilt offering	reparation offering

(WBC: *Word Biblical Commentary*)

Leviticus 1—7: laws about sacrifices

Chapters 1—7 of Leviticus deal with various types of sacrifice. These are:

Ch. 1	Burnt offering (or whole-burnt offering; of holocaust—that is, the whole animal was burnt)
Ch. 2	Cereal offering (or grain offering)
Ch. 3	Peace offering (or sacrifice of well-being)
Chs. 4:1—5:13	Sin offering (or purification offering)
Chs. 5:14—6:7	Guilt offering (or reparation offering)
Chs. 6:8—7:36	Rituals of burnt offering (6:8–13), cereal offering (6:14–18), consecration of priests (6:19–23), sin offering (6:24–30), guilt offering (7:1–10), peace offering, including votive and free-will offerings (7:11–36, including regulations about uncleanness).
Ch. 7:37f	Summary statement (thus the rituals for burnt offering, cereal offering, sin offering, guilt offering, peace offering as God commanded Moses).

Chiasmus and chiastic structures

A chiasmus is a literary device whereby words, phrases, ideas and so on are repeated in reverse order around a central pivot. The structure is often indicated by letters, for example, a-b-b-a or a-b-b'-a'. A simple example would be:

a   The Lord
b   is great
b' wonderful
a' are his deeds

If we arrange this differently, you can see how the name 'chiasmus' (from the Greek letter chi = X) comes about:

$$\begin{matrix} \text{The Lord} & \searrow \nearrow & \text{wonderful} \\ \text{is great} & \nearrow \searrow & \text{are his deeds} \end{matrix}$$

This device is found many times in the Bible and it serves to indicate certain features of a text, most often with a more complicated form, for example, a-b-c-b-a, or a-b-c-d-c-b-a.

1. It marks the beginning and end of a unit, something that has a certain coherence in itself.

2. It often places the most important idea, or the turning point in a unit, at the centre point.

3. The ending is in some way similar to the beginning, quite often transformed to a new situation.

A very simplified outline of Zechariah 7—8 provides us with a quite sophisticated illustration:

a Some men came from Bethel to 'entreat the favour of the Lord'.
   b They brought a question about fasting.
      c Zechariah challenges them: fasting? Remember why you are in this state: you didn't heed the words of the prophets.
         d God is going to reverse the judgment, and again dwell in Jerusalem as your God, with you as his people.
      c So from now on, keep the words previously given by the former prophets.
   b And your fasts will become feasts.
a And in the future, people will come from all over the world to 'entreat the favour of the Lord'.

Right in the middle of this whole section is the most important expression of the purpose of God in the Old Testament: 'I will be your God and you will be my people.' And notice how the depressing, small-scale, seeking the Lord's will about fasting is transformed into a universal seeking the Lord with rejoicing.

There are examples of chiastic structures in Leviticus and Numbers (for example, Leviticus 22:10–13; 24:14–23). Note the way that the structure brings out the coherence of the unit and the progression of thought, often marking, at the centre, a turning point or special emphasis.

FURTHER READING AND REFERENCE

Short, accessible commentaries and books

Raymond Brown, *The Message of Numbers* (Bible Speaks Today series) (IVP, 2002). Written with an emphasis on what the book teaches and its relevance for today.

R.K. Harrison, *Leviticus* (Tyndale Old Testament Commentaries) (IVP, 1980). Handy and helpful.

Derek Kidner, *Leviticus—Deuteronomy* (Bible Study Books) (Scripture Union, 1971). Long out of print but a little gem and worth picking up second-hand.

Derek Tidball, *Discovering Leviticus* (Crossway Bible Guides) (Crossway, 1996). A popular treatment of Leviticus with many helpful insights and ideas.

Gordon J. Wenham, *The Book of Numbers* (Tyndale Old Testament Commentaries) (IVP, 1981). Handy and helpful.

More technical commentaries and books

Timothy R. Ashley, *Numbers* (New International Commentary on the Old Testament) (Eerdmans, 1993).

Philip J. Budd, *Leviticus* (New Century Bible) (Eerdmans, 1996).

Philip J. Budd, *Numbers* (Word Biblical Commentary) (Word, 1984).

R.K. Harrison, 'Leper; Leprosy' in *International Standard Bible Encyclopedia*, vol. 3, p. 105.

John E. Hartley, *Leviticus* (Word Biblical Commentary) (Word, 1992).

J.R. Porter, *Leviticus* (Cambridge Bible Commentary) (CUP, 1976).

N.H. Snaith, *Leviticus and Numbers* (New Century Bible) (Oliphants/Marshall, Morgan and Scott, 1971). Now old and out of print but still useful.

Gordon J. Wenham, *The Book of Leviticus* (New International Commentary on the Old Testament) (Eerdmans, 1979). A detailed, scholarly, useful commentary.

Other books

T. Desmond Alexander, *From Paradise to the Promised Land* (Paternoster, 1995). A traditional approach that relates the themes of the Pentateuch to each other and shows how the whole of it holds together.

Roger T. Beckwith and Martin J. Selman (eds.), *Sacrifice in the Bible* (Paternoster, 1995). Contains some useful articles for those who want to investigate aspects of 'sacrifice' in the Old and New Testaments in more detail.

T.E. Fretheim, *The Pentateuch* (Abingdon, 1996). A stimulating book that advances a reader-response approach, but guards against 'anything goes' interpretation by giving careful attention to historical matters.

Paula Gooder, *The Pentateuch. A Story of Beginnings* (Continuum, 2000). A brief introductory book for students.

John W. Rogerson, R.W.L. Moberly and William Johnstone, *Genesis and Exodus* (with an Introduction by John Goldingay) (Sheffield Academic Press, 2001). Intended for college and seminary use, but clear and readable. The introduction is especially helpful and contains much that is relevant to the whole Pentateuch

The MISSION of the SPIES (NUMBERS 13) & the BORDERS of CANAAN (NUMBERS 34)

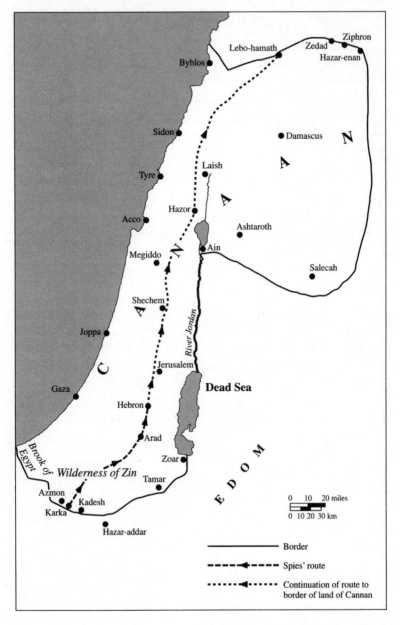

The ROUTE *of the* ISRAELITES
from EGYPT *to* MOAB (NUMBERS 33)

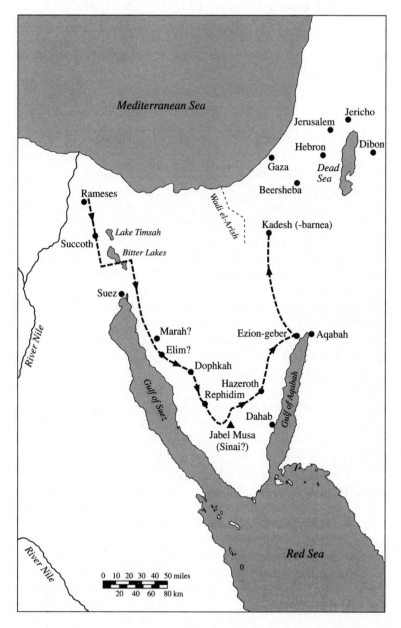

1   LEVITICUS 1

EVERYTHING UP IN SMOKE

Leviticus 1:1–2 gives a general introduction to sacrifice: livestock offerings are to be from herd or flock. (You may also offer birds or crops, actually.)

Verses 3–17 describe the laws concerning burnt offerings: herd (vv. 3–9); flock (vv. 10–13); birds (vv. 14–17).

Sacrifice: two important points

'You shall lay your hand on the head of the burnt offering, and it shall be acceptable in your behalf as atonement for you' (v. 4).

There is a deep-seated human feeling that sacrifices need to be offered. The motivation for this is varied: it may be to turn away the anger of the deity, to express sorrow for sin and to make restitution, to receive forgiveness, to gain power, to express gratitude to God. Thus the Bible has something in common with many other religions from different regions and different eras. It also differs from at least some others in two important ways. First, God does not encourage people to make up their own rituals: they are presented as God's initiative; they are laid out in detail and must be followed exactly. Second, they are not a means of coercing God to do something for the one who brings a sacrifice.

Sacrifices emphasize two important theological points. Sin against God is as serious as anything can be. He is holy and will not tolerate disobedience. There is nothing a person can do that will make good a lapse from doing God's will. *But* God in his grace *does* forgive people their sins and restores them to fellowship with him. This is to be achieved according to his requirements and not ours.

Many have taken offence at this sort of emphasis. They assume that anything well-meant should be accepted by God—but why should we ever assume this? The way God views the world and our actions is not self-evident. Suppose a drunken driver had knocked over and killed a young child. Would the driver send a box of chocolates (or even a shoulder of beef) with a note to say sorry? Would they expect any gift at all to be acceptable? Surely most of our sins are not like that—but how *does* God regard them? He alone can tell us.

The meaning of the 'holocaust'

The whole burnt offering (sometimes called the 'holocaust') is introduced without saying why or when it is to be offered. However, it is prescribed for various rituals as we read further in Leviticus and Numbers, and we can deduce from this that it is basically a gift to God associated with making atonement for sin (9:7; 16:24). Often a burnt offering was offered alongside other types of sacrifice: for example, in Leviticus 5:7 two birds are offered, the first as a sin offering and the second as a burnt offering.

Some scholars believe that the burnt offering signified total self-committal to God. Laying one's hand upon the animal would indicate identification with the animal—and what was about to happen to it. Some interpret the 'hand-on' act to indicate that atonement is the main concern. Still others believe that there is a general witness to the fact that approaching God requires atonement and/or appeasement. As you come across further references to burnt offerings. ask yourself the questions, 'What does this have to do with gifts/gratitude, atonement/appeasement and commitment/consecration to God?'

Whatever may be the precise intention of each burnt offering, the worshipper should have had assurance that the sacrifice was provided by God. Therefore, rightly offered, God would accept it. Therefore, God would accept the worshipper.

FOR MEDITATION AND PRAYER

Do I find myself wanting to express my joy in Christ or my gratitude to him? Do I ever catch myself slipping into trying to appease God or get round him in some way?

O God, we praise you for the sacrifice to end all sacrifices, the gift of your only Son, our Saviour, Jesus Christ. We offer you a sacrifice of praise and a life lived for your glory. Through Jesus Christ our Lord. Amen.

2 LEVITICUS 2 (i)

NON-MEAT SACRIFICES

Chapter 1 dealt with 'burnt offerings' or 'whole burnt offerings'. We shall see them referred to in connection with a number of different rituals as we proceed through Leviticus. The sacrifice could be a bull, ram, billy-goat, turtle dove or pigeon, and the whole was burnt. Grain offerings were made of flour and oil with accompanying frankincense, and only a part of them was burnt—though 'all its frankincense' was to be burnt (vv. 2, 16). The remainder went to the priests, 'Aaron's sons'.

Women sacrifice too?

Verse 1 begins, 'When a soul or person...', that is, 'When anyone, male or female...' Verbs in Hebrew have to be either masculine or feminine, but the masculine is used when the subject is 'he or she'. In this sentence we have: 'When a *nephesh* ('soul'—a feminine noun) brings (feminine verb)... of choice flour shall be *his* offering.' It is interesting that an inclusive word is chosen, since only males were *commanded* to appear before the Lord three times a year (Exodus 23:17). In Herod's temple (but not Solomon's or the 'Second Temple') there was a Court of Women, outside the Court of Israel and the Court of Priests. Men could proceed as far as the altar but women could not. The regulations in Leviticus suggest that this development was not originally intended, and the command for males to come to the sanctuary *allowed* the women to stay behind and take care of necessary matters (like seeing to the animals). It also seems obvious that the priests' families would have to have eaten from the priests' portions, since that was how the priests were supported and they, in turn, had to support their families.

The attitudes towards women that are reflected in the earliest period of Israel's history seem to be rather different from those that developed later. Moses' sister Miriam was a prophet (Exodus 15: 20–21). In the period of the judges, Deborah was a woman with both political and spiritual authority (see Judges 4—5). Huldah the prophetess was consulted in preference to the young Jeremiah when the lost book of the law was rediscovered (2 Kings 22:14–20). There are several other significant women in the Old Testament and there is no sense of their being inferior or denigrated in the way that we find in Ecclesiasticus (Sirach): '...for from garments comes the moth, and from a woman comes woman's wickedness. Better is the wickedness of a man than a woman who does good; and it is a woman who brings shame and disgrace (42:13–14). Christian history also knows of lapses into unbiblical and unhealthy attitudes towards women.

Some argue today that men and women are equal but are meant to have different roles, so it is not surprising that some positions are for men only. Sometimes this looks rather like saying that the boss and the office boy are equal but have different functions, but is it necessarily a sexist view? How can we identify and take action against our own prejudices?

Vegetarians not second class

Verses 14–16 refer to offering the first fruits of the grain. This always signified something special: the contrast between Abel's sacrifice and Cain's was that Abel 'brought of the firstlings of his flock, their fat portions', whereas Cain simply brought 'an offering' (Genesis 4:3–4). There is no suggestion in Genesis that grain offerings are second rate, let alone unacceptable, and Leviticus 2 confirms this. Throughout Leviticus we shall see an emphasis on right attitude, whether expressed explicitly or not—a concern that worshippers approach God by the means that he has appointed and in the manner that he requires. The rabbis interpreted the reference to 'a soul' as meaning that the grain offering represents the worshipper's whole self.

FOR REFLECTION

Genesis 9:3–4 allows non-vegetarianism, but the ideal seems to be portrayed in Isaiah 11:6–7. Are we intended to move towards that ideal here and now?

3   LEVITICUS 2 (ii)

NON-MEAT OFFERINGS & THEIR TRIMMINGS

As we noted when we considered Leviticus 1, the non-meat sacrifices are carefully stipulated. All consist of grain with oil, and all have frankincense spread on them. Frankincense is a balsamic resin obtained from certain shrubs that were found in Sheba (Isaiah 60:6; Jeremiah 6:20) and may or may not have been native to Palestine. It was burnt as perfume (Song of Solomon 3:6; 4:6, 14). In Psalm 141:2 the psalmist asks that his prayer might be as incense—that is, as something that is known to be acceptable to God. The use of frankincense was forbidden, however, in the case of the sin offering (Leviticus 5:11).

Forbidden: salt and sweeteners

Salt was always to be offered (v. 13); leaven (yeast) never (v. 11). Sweeteners like honey were also strictly excluded (the word translated 'honey' in verse 11 is probably a more general word for sweet substances including honey). There were, however, certain allowed variations. The worshipper could make a basic cake with the flour and oil or a flatter wafer (presumably with less oil) and spread oil on it. The cake or wafer would then be baked in an oven (v. 4). It seems likely that the method was to pre-heat the cylindrical clay oven by lighting a fire inside, and then to stick the cake against the inside wall, a method apparently still used in some regions today—and probably similar to tandoori cooking?

On the other hand, the cake could be cooked on a flat iron, pan or griddle (vv. 5–6; we are not sure of the exact meaning of the Hebrew word used), or they could cook it in a pan (v. 7)—that is, deep-fry it, producing something like a diabetic doughnut. I wonder if the priest may have been allowed to spread honey on what came to him after the Lord's portion had been offered. Probably not.

We are not sure of the significance of all these instructions. The text does not tell us, and so we do not know whose guesses are the best. For example, why the detail about the different kinds of cakes? Could it be to provide some variety for the priests who depended upon portions of the sacrifices for their livelihood? Could it be to exclude outlandish recipes of some sort? Or did it simply authorize ordinary, common food—the types of cake that people regularly made?

Leaven and honey were forbidden: both cause fermentation, but they also improve flavour, texture and edibility. It is only later that leaven is referred to as something bad. Even in the New Testament, leaven in itself is neutral: the kingdom of God spreads like leaven, gradually pervading the whole of creation (for example, Matthew 13:33), but the disciples are to beware of 'the leaven of the Pharisees' (Mark 8:15) and the early Christians were told to 'purge out the old leaven' (1 Corinthians 5:6–8). The reason for requiring salt may be similar: it spreads and *preserves* the whole lump. We also know, however, that bread without salt tastes horrible—to most people. Either way, it provides a useful parable for Christians: 'you are the salt of the earth' (Matthew 5:13). Irrespective of the symbolic reason, scholars believe that there was a long tradition that eating salt together establishes a personal bond, and this idea is still prevalent among Arabs today.

Sacrifices: God's initiative

The sacrifices of the Old Testament are to be thought of as God's reaching out to us, providing us with a means of reaching him. We could perhaps think of a bridge that we may cross with confidence since it has been constructed by the chief engineer. The grain offering particularly encourages us to trust that we may offer what is ordinary or common. When God authorizes such things, they are acceptable and special.

FOR REFLECTION AND PRAYER

What can I give you, poor as I am?
What I have I give you—give my heart.

After Christina Rossetti (1830–94),
from the hymn 'In the bleak midwinter'

EATING *with* GOD

Having dealt with (whole) burnt offerings (ch. 1) and vegetarian offerings (cereal or meal offerings, ch. 2) Leviticus goes on to describe 'peace offerings' or 'fellowship offerings' or 'offerings of well-being'. We are not told the significance of these offerings any more than the previous ones. We have to look at the meaning of the word used and pick up clues from the way that peace offerings are commanded for various differing situations later in Leviticus. The first seven chapters of Leviticus, in fact, are a manual for priests, rather like a computer manual which might, for instance, tell you how to write a letter, but would not suggest reasons for writing a letter.

The word 'peace offering' (*shelem*) comes from the same root as *shalom*, which means 'peace, completeness, wholeness, soundness, welfare', and it signifies a sacrifice for alliance or friendship. It is used in conjunction with and in contrast to 'whole burnt offerings' in various contexts where there is a public solemn ritual or a celebration of some sort. For example, see Exodus 24:5, where Moses and the people ratify the covenant that God has graciously made with them; and Exodus 32:6, where they followed, no doubt, the usual practice but with a completely wrong focus.

How to do it

The instructions are given three times: for a cow or bull (vv. 1–5), a sheep (vv. 6–11) and a goat (vv. 12–16). The main differences are that the sheep's fat tail is specifically mentioned; it is not specified that the goat may be male or female (but presumably it could), and there are slight differences in wording between verses 5, 11 and 16.

The procedure is similar to other sacrifices.

The worshipper brings the animal to the entrance of the tent of meeting, lays his* hand on its head and kills it (* or presumably 'her hand': the norm would be for a man to offer sacrifices on behalf of his whole family, but the Bible often allows for exceptions without specifying them).

The exact significance of this 'laying on of hands' is not entirely clear. As with church members today, no doubt there would have been many different understandings, some of them quite vague, concerning the action. It would seem, though, that some sort of identification with the victim must have been supposed: 'This is *my* sacrifice. What happens to it has significance for me.' See also Numbers 8:10–19, where laying hands on the heads of the Levites by the people signifies that the Levites *take the place of* the firstborn of all the Israelites.

The priests dash blood against the altar. Since the blood signifies the life (or the life that has now ceased), this action would indicate that the animal has been killed and offered to God. Only the priests can approach the altar, since they are especially authorized and it is God who decides on how he might be approached.

The worshipper offers the fat, the kidneys and the appendage of the liver as a sacrifice. God has first claim on the sacrifice, and the parts that must be burnt are specified here (no reason is given for the choice of these parts). The rest was returned to the worshipper for a celebration meal in the presence of the Lord.

The priests 'turn these into smoke' on the altar:

- with the burnt offering (v. 5, with offerings 'from the herd' only)
- as an offering by fire (vv. 11 and 16, 'as a food offering')
- for a pleasing odour to the Lord (vv. 5, 16)

Unstated: then we all have a great feast!

Holy Communion offerings

Peace offerings have the most obvious connection with the Christian celebration of Holy Communion. Worshippers eat (and drink) in the presence of God, receiving by faith the benefits of the body of Christ, the Prince of Peace. There are differences too: Christians do not offer a burnt offering, a sin offering or any other kind of sacrifice for sin, since their high priest, Jesus Christ himself, has already offered that one perfect sacrifice (see Hebrews 9:11–14, 26–28; 10:10–14).

FOR REFLECTION AND PRAYER

'Rejoice before the Lord—you and your sons and your daughters,
your male and female slaves… strangers, orphans, widows…'
(Deuteronomy 16:11). Has rejoicing before the Lord given way
to other forms of celebration? Can we find a way of enjoying
wholeheartedly and enthusiastically the material blessings
of life without forgetting the Provider?

5 LEVITICUS 4:1–12

UNINTENTIONAL SIN

The scope of the sin offering

It comes as a shock to most people to realize how limited a provision was made in the Old Testament to deal with sin (vv. 1–2). The sin offering can only cope with unintentional sins. Sins 'with a high hand' are explicitly excluded from cover by sacrifices in Numbers 15:30–31. We realize, of course, that certain crimes had penalties prescribed, including the death penalty for murder, striking or cursing father or mother, kidnapping, sorcery, bestiality and idolatry, adultery, and leading people astray from the Lord (Exodus 21:12, 15–17; 22:18–20; Leviticus 20:10; Deuteronomy 13:5). But what was the position with in-between sins, those that were deliberate but not as serious as those mentioned above? What if a man deliberately struck his wife? What about deliberately stealing money? And what about the unintentional sins of which the sinner remains unaware?

Common sense must have been needed to fill some of these gaps (for example, a rude remark would not, presumably, have called for a sacrifice), along with principles laid out elsewhere in the Law. Repentance and restitution (Exodus 22:1–6, 12–15) are implied or explicitly stated in many passages of the Old Testament. The sacrificial system, therefore, is shown here to be incomplete in a number of ways. Forgiveness is basically due to God's grace, but the strict prescriptions attached to sacrifices demonstrate the seriousness of opposing or neglecting God's requirements.

Although not mentioned explicitly here, it is obvious that repentance, that is, turning away from the wrongdoing, is a prerequisite for offering an acceptable sacrifice. The Day of Atonement dealt with the unknown sins of all the people (see comment on Leviticus 16, pp. 72–75).

This all seems to indicate that what really matters is actual relationships with God and other human beings, and confirms Jesus' insight in naming the two greatest commandments: 'You shall love the Lord your God with all your heart...' and 'You shall love your neighbour as yourself' (Deuteronomy 6:5; Leviticus 19:18).

The anointed priest's sin offering

The first section of verses 3–12 deals with the actions of the priest who has sinned, 'thus bringing guilt on the people' (v. 3). We shall deal with similar actions for the whole congregation, a ruler, and an 'ordinary person' in the next reading. The action is set out below together with brief notes, to make clearer the essentials of what used to happen. The expression 'anointed priest' is odd, since all priests were anointed, but it may indicate the high priest.

The priest who has sinned takes a bull, and lays his hand on its head (identifying himself with what is happening to the bull). The bull is killed before the Lord (presumably by the priest himself). Then the priest brings the blood to the tent of meeting, where he:

- sprinkles some of it with his finger seven times before the curtain of the sanctuary, that is, the holy of holies
- puts some blood on the horns of the altar of incense (which was inside the tent)
- pours out the rest of the blood at the base of the altar of burnt offering (which was outside the tent)
- burns the fat (as for the peace offering) on the altar of burnt offering
- burns the skin, flesh, head, legs, entrails, and dung on the ash heap outside the camp.

This probably seems like a very messy practice to those of us who are not used to slaughterhouses and the like. In terms of health, the regulations of the Old Testament probably did a great deal to prevent disease. Even more important, in the context of ancient society, it represents the regulation of one well-known aspect of life, that is, killing for food, and its transformation into something that could speak powerfully of the deepest religious concerns.

FOR REFLECTION

If it is true that God starts where people are, what contemporary beliefs, assumptions and practices provide a good starting point for teaching about relationships with God?

SINS *of* PEOPLE & LEADERS

The second part of this chapter deals with three further classes of 'sinner'. The procedure is basically the same as that outlined for the priest in verses 3–12, but there are a few additional details and a few variations. For example, the blood of the sin offering is put on the horns of the altar of incense (inside the tent) in the case of the anointed priest and the whole congregation (4:7, 18), but for the ruler or ordinary person it is put on the horns of the altar of burnt offering outside the tent (vv. 25, 30).

The whole congregation has sinned

There is a puzzle here in verse 20, where it says, 'He shall do with the bull just as is done with the bull of sin offering'. But this *is* the bull of sin offering. Is it a mistake for peace offering (as in v. 10) or does it simply mean 'as is done with the sin offering for a priest'? That seems more likely.

An important word occurs in verse 20: 'make atonement'. The word (one word in Hebrew, *kipper*) comes from the root that is known from the phrase *Yom Kippur*, day of atonement. The priest makes atonement for the people and 'they shall be forgiven'. The word 'atonement' is a specially coined English word formed from the phrase 'at-one'. In other words, 'atonement' is that which causes people who are at odds with each other to be 'at one'. This does not explain the ideas that lie behind the Hebrew understanding, but some clues may be gleaned from a few observations.

The word may be derived from a verbal root meaning 'cover' (compare Jeremiah 18:23), signifying the covering over of sins. Or it may be derived from the word 'ransom', which was used for the price paid in order to buy a slave's freedom (Exodus 21:30; Job 33:24; 36:18; Proverbs 13:8). The ransom money was paid to the slave owner, either by the slave or another person, and the slave was free. This metaphor is important in the New Testament for describing the results of Christ's death, as in Mark 10:45—'to give his life as a ransom for many'. A price is paid and we are freed from enslavement to sin. Pressing the metaphor too far in demanding to know who receives the ransom has led to much unedifying theological discussion!

The notion of the sin of a whole people is unfashionable today. Yet there are echoes of it in various places, for example, in the growing (I hope) realization that the countries of 'the north' as a whole have exploited 'the south' and that, therefore, it is right and just to correct structures that maintain this injustice. The campaigns to persuade governments to cancel Third World debt express this concern in action. Days of national and international repentance might be the natural successor to the sacrifices described here.

A ruler or prince has sinned

In sacrifices for the sin of a ruler (vv. 22–26), it is a male goat that is specified, and the blood is put upon the horns of the altar of burnt offering (not the altar of incense, compare vv. 7, 18 with 25, 30). Otherwise the ritual is basically the same. The type of ruler is not defined precisely but none is excluded—not even the king. This is also clear from various prophetic texts (for example, 1 Kings 21:19; Isaiah 39:5–7; Amos 7:11, 16–17). On the other hand, several kings do not receive the treatment prescribed by the Law for their sins. No doubt, on a practical level, this was because they had too much power. There are, however, hints that God overruled the punishment due in certain cases (2 Samuel 12:11–14; 1 Kings 21:27–29).

One of the common people has sinned

The sin of a common person (vv. 27–35) requires a female goat (v. 28) or a ewe lamb (v. 32). No explanation is given for the details. We might suppose that common people did not keep male goats or that a male goat would better symbolize a leader, but these are mere speculations. The main point is that God has the prerogative to specify what he likes and we are expected to obey.

The New Testament takes up the image of carrying the parts that are not burnt on the altar to a place 'outside the camp' (4:12, 21). Hebrews 13:11–16 links it with the fact that Jesus 'suffered outside the city gate in order to sanctify the people through his own blood'. The region outside the camp was regarded as 'unclean' but Jesus has sanctified it.

FOR PRAYER

Lord, forgive the sins of church and nation of which we are a part.
Help us to work for policies that make for justice and harmony.
In the name of the Prince of Peace. Amen.

7 LEVITICUS 5:1–13

The SCOPE *of* SIN OFFERINGS

At last we have some concrete examples of what the sin offering should be used to compensate for (vv. 1–4): failing to testify when publicly called to do so, touching an unclean carcass of some kind, touching human uncleanness, and making a rash oath.

There is something puzzling again because we find references in verses 6 and 7 to both 'sin offering' and a word (*asham*) that can mean 'guilt offering' (as in 5:14ff). Two explanations are possible. First, since the word can also mean 'guilt' or 'penalty' (NRSV), this is its meaning in verses 6–7: 'he shall bring a sin offering as a *penalty*'. Second, verses 1–13 refer to the sin offering and round off the previous section. The section seems to be constructed like this:

Verses 1–4   Actions that require a sin offering in order to make atonement.

Verses 5–6   Recap: what an ordinary person brings as a sin offering (a female lamb or goat).

Verses 7–10 Special provision for a poorer person: two birds (turtle doves or pigeons)

Verses 11–13 Special provision for an even poorer person (cereal offering; see comment on Leviticus 2, pp. 30–31)

The actions that require a sin offering are a strange mixture at first sight. Some seem to be comparatively trivial to modern ways of thinking, but they have deep implications. Consideration of the Old Testament concern could stimulate us to more responsible citizenship today.

False witness is forbidden by the ninth commandment and stands for all forms of lying. Witnesses were highly significant in the discovering of truth and the administration of justice among the people of Israel. There was no police force, although there were elders who acted as judges, and there was no developed system of interrogation for sorting out the truth from lies and prevarication. False witnesses could bring about an innocent person's death—as indeed they still can. Recognizing this, the law forbade the death penalty based on one witness alone (Numbers 35:30). The aw assumes that God will not intervene directly to point out the guilty and expects people to use sensible safeguards and common sense—or even uncommon wisdom (1 Kings 3:16–28)! So keeping quiet could lead to a miscarriage of justice. Presumably someone who realized they had failed in their duty to testify would need to put this right as far as possible before bringing the sin offering.

The next sins specified are ritual in nature. A person who touched the carcass of an unclean animal, such as a pig or camel (11:1–8), or a clean animal that had become unclean (for example, by being left over from a sacrifice on the second or third day: 7:15, 18), or an unclean 'swarming thing'. The last named included small reptiles and quadrupeds (such as weasel, mouse and lizard: 11:29–30) and insects (Deuteronomy 14:19). Human uncleanness refers to bodily fluids as in Leviticus 15.

The last example given is of making a rash vow. Jephthah was guilty of this, and neither he nor his daughter had the confidence to seek release from the vow (Judges 11:34–36). He was a leader in Israel, but certainly not because of his theological understanding, and the end of the book of Judges gives the verdict over the whole period: 'In those days there was no king… all the people did what was right in their own eyes'. Other examples of rash vows might perhaps be to do with actions that are actually wrong, such as, 'I vow to make a graven image of…' or 'If you plough up my barley again, I'll kill you'. Better to realize the sin of the rash vow than the sin of carrying out what is vowed.

Verses 5–13 show that God is sensitive to people's ability to offer sacrifices to him and that poverty does not disqualify a person from approaching the Lord. In the case of the cereal offering, we note that there is no blood required, and this provides the exception alluded to in Hebrews 9:22: 'almost everything is purified with blood'.

The whole section on sin offerings demonstrates very clearly an emphasis that we will see frequently throughout the Bible—the seriousness of being careless about God's requirements and his readiness to restore us to fellowship with him. These concerns, made surer and clearer in the New Testament, are already set out in the Old.

FOR REFLECTION

The death of Christ, the most important death in the history of the world, was assisted by false witnesses. Did they thereby provide their own sin offering?

OFFERINGS: GUILT *or* REPARATION?

The next section goes on to deal with something we have not met
previously—the guilt offering. The actual distinction between this
and the sin offering is difficult to work out. There must be a close
connection because the sin offering is prescribed in order to deal with
guilt. Both are given for the purpose of making atonement (Leviticus
4; also 5:6, 10, 13, 16, 18; 6:7) and the ritual is the same (7:7). So
did they really need two separate types of sacrifice?

There are two main suggestions concerning the scope of the guilt
offering. The first is that it was to deal with offences where restitution
was possible. Some scholars therefore give it the term 'reparation
offering'. This aspect is certainly present in Leviticus 5:16 and 6:5.
The second suggestion is that it was prescribed for the violation of
anything sacred, as is indicated by 5:15–16. The latter would not
cover all offences listed, for 6:2ff concerns sins against other people.
So perhaps it was prescribed for the two types of offence separately.

The structure is as follows.

5:14–15 Those who sin with respect to a 'holy thing' must bring a
ram as a guilt offering.

5:16   If restitution is appropriate, it must be given with a 20 per
cent surcharge. This presumably applies if the guilty person
has stolen, lost or damaged something.

5:17–19 Those who do what the Lord has forbidden are guilty, even
if they do not know they have transgressed, and they must
offer a guilt offering. The text does not mention anything
about the person coming to realize a fault. One must
assume it, as in 4:14, 23, 28.

6:1–7   Those who deceive or cheat their neighbours must restore
what has been lost, plus 20 per cent.

Notice that such an action against a neighbour is described as a
breach of faith *against the Lord* (6:2). This is one of the notable
differences between Old Testament law and laws that have been
found in other cultures in ancient west Asia. For example, if a man

committed adultery with a married woman, in other cultures her husband had the power to decide the fate of them both. We have texts which allow the wronged man to put them both to death or to mutilate them both (for example, by cutting off the wife's nose and castrating the man and mutilating his face), or to waive the penalty. He had to treat both equally. In Israel, adultery was a sin against the Lord and the Lord decided the penalty (death—which Jesus, in effect, commuted: see John 8:3–11).

There are examples in other cultures of having to pay back more than was stolen. For instance, in Hittite law we find, 'If anyone steals a ewe or ram, they used to give formerly twelve sheep. Now he shall give six sheep…'. They seem to be trying to find the right penalty.

A question has been raised about how a sin can be hidden and then come to be known—'when you have sinned and realize your guilt' (6:4). This applies to several sections. For example, if the high priest sinned inadvertently (4:3), how would he find out his need to make a sin offering?

- It might simply be that someone else notices (for example, that he has touched a corpse without realizing it) and tells him.

- He might learn something later on about the status of meat given to him.

- His conscience might prompt him to ask whether he has dealt fairly with another person.

- He might be prompted to seek the Lord through Urim and Thummim, a way of receiving a 'yes–no' decision in response to a specific question put to God. Perhaps the clearest example is in 1 Samuel 23:9–12, where two specific questions receive a 'yes' answer.

- He might pray (perhaps because of a disaster, presumed to be God's judgment) and have it revealed to him, as in the case of David in 2 Samuel 21:1.

FOR REFLECTION

It was assumed in ancient times that disasters were sent by God for a specific purpose. Job makes it clear that this is not invariably so.
But does God try to get through to us sometimes by events that happen to us? What might cause you to 'seek the Lord' today? How would you receive an answer—and know that you have received it?

FOUR RITUALS

The structure of the next three sections is clear. We have details concerning the rituals for the sacrifices mentioned so far, then a new one,
(the wave offering or elevation offering), followed by a summary.

The (whole) burnt offering

We have had information in Leviticus 1 about the burnt offering, the
offering that was completely consumed by fire. But in 7:8, we read
that the priest shall have the skin of a burnt offering! This illustrates
the principle that 'exceptions may be allowed for but not stated'. This
does not seem quite logical to us, but we need to accept that this is
the way the Hebrew Bible (that is, the Protestant Old Testament, the
Bible accepted by Jews today) puts things. Further examples are
found in connection with the spies (where God says in Numbers
14:22–24 that none shall enter Canaan except Caleb, but it is understood that Joshua is also an exception), and in giving prophecies: 'Set
your house in order, for you shall die; you shall not recover', but [not
stated] 'if you beseech me to grant you an extension, you won't die'
(2 Kings 20:1–7).

The fire burning all night would make sure that the burnt offering,
which had to remain there, was completely consumed. No remnants
would be left to distract from the symbolism of something wholly
offered to God. Strict regulations are given even for the priest's under-
wear, all emphasizing the need for purity and the dangers of approaching a holy God carelessly. In these clothes only, the priest was to
remove the ashes of the burnt offering from the altar. Then, wearing
ordinary clothes, he would carry them 'outside the camp'—but to a
clean place. There is here implied a progression from holiness (contact
with the altar and so on) to cleanness to uncleanness (defiled by
corpses, for example). The continually burning altar fire might also
signify that the lines to God were always open (vv. 12–13).

The cereal or grain offering

Leviticus 2 has already given the recipes for cereal offerings and some
instructions. Here we are told that Aaron and his sons, that is, the
priests, are to eat their portion in a holy place (v. 16), that all *male*

descendants of Aaron are to eat it as their due, and that everything that touches them becomes holy (v. 18).

Verses 19–23 give instructions about the cereal offerings of the high priest, on the day when he is anointed. The quantity (one tenth of an ephah) is stated and the cooking options are limited. With the cereal offerings of ordinary people, the priest, in his capacity as God's representative, burnt a portion and ate the rest. In the case of his own offerings, the distinction between himself and God is in focus and there is no reason for him to retain part for his own consumption.

The sin and guilt offerings

To the information of Leviticus 4 is added instruction on what to do in the case of blood spattering on the clothes (they are to be washed in a holy place), and how to guard against remnants of blood in cooking vessels (vv. 27–28). Verse 30 refers to sin offerings for the high priest or the community. The high priest (and therefore everyone else too) was forbidden to eat any of this offering, quite possibly because in each case the priest was himself implicated in the sin, either as mediator or as a member of the whole community (4:3, 6, 13, 17).

The ritual for the guilt offering (7:1–10) is very similar to the sin offering, as verse 7 makes clear. We have seen most of this information previously but there is a further regulation concerning, in effect, the fees paid for actually performing a ritual (v. 9) and those that go towards maintaining the priesthood.

The New Testament refers to these provisions as 'wages' in Luke 10:7 and 1 Timothy 5:18 ('labourers deserve their wages'). Kidner comments, '…the recipients are given the security of a fixed share, as of right… God may test his servants by shortage, but he does not show a preference for pauperizing them' (p. 10).

FOR REFLECTION

*Rituals to stimulate sight, smell, hearing, touch and taste:
are we missing out?*

THREE KINDS *of* PEACE OFFERING

We are here given the sort of reference that tells you the writer assumes that you know more than you actually do: '*if* your offering of well-being (peace offering) is for thanksgiving...'. Ah, so there are different reasons for making a peace offering! The ones given here are as a thank offering, a votive offering or a freewill offering.

As a thanksgiving or thank offering

It's often quite difficult to know exactly what 'thanksgiving' is in Western culture. Sometimes it simply means 'saying thank you to be polite' and possibly showing respect in a vague sort of way. In Hebrew thought, there is a greater emphasis on praise and a more conscious directing of praise towards God, the giver of benefits received. So the meaning is basically 'praise for particular blessings'.

It is easy to see that a fellowship celebration meal in God's presence—that is, a peace offering—would be just the thing for this. For the Israelites, there seems to have been no problem in having a 'solemn assembly' along with exuberant praise—and no problem for God either, who requires simply that the worshippers approach in the 'right state'. This is expressed in various ways: they must be 'clean' (v. 19)—that is, ritually clean, not having touched a corpse or any form of unclean creature or substance, nor having disobeyed God's regulations and thereby shown a lack of respect for the holy God. The prophets give us yet deeper insight into what disqualifies a person from approaching God, even when they have the right offerings—namely unrighteous behaviour, including especially oppression of the poor, and idolatry (Amos 4:4–5; 5:22–23).

As a vow or votive offering

Making vows seems to be a natural instinct for human beings, and the earliest parts of the Bible contain references to it. For example, Jacob vows, after his vision and God's promise to him (Genesis 28:20), 'If God will be with me, and will keep me... so that I come again to my father's house in peace, then the Lord shall be my God...'. At the end of many of the psalms of distress, the psalmist vows to praise God 'in the midst of the congregation' (see especially Psalm 22:22–25;

compare Psalm 7:17; 13:6; 26:12). No doubt there is a danger that this may lead to trying to make a bargain with God, but it can also be a way of expressing amazement and gratitude in the face of God's gracious action. This passage indicates that peace offerings were a natural thing to vow (and were then called 'votive offerings') or a natural accompaniment to the fulfilment of a vow.

As a freewill offering

The word used means 'voluntariness' and these are offerings given solely from a desire to give to God, perhaps for particular blessings received, perhaps for a special project that inspires the giver, such as the erection and furnishing of the tabernacle (Exodus 35:29; 36:3) or temple (2 Chronicles 31:14; Ezra 1:4; 8:28). Most often the votive offering would take the form of a sacrifice, and Ezekiel 46:12 tells us that this could be either a (whole) burnt offering or a peace offering.

The instructions given for offering the peace offering assume what has been prescribed in Leviticus 3 and require the addition of four kinds of cereal offering or grain offering. To the two described in Leviticus 2:4 are added 'cakes of choice flour well soaked in oil' (v. 12) and 'cakes of *leavened* bread' (v. 13). It appears that the worshipper was to bring all four ('and' v. 12). The reason for the leavened bread is not hinted at.

The peace offering was to be eaten on the same day if it was a thank offering, otherwise by the second day. The variation suggests that this was not simply a matter of health and hygiene. Possibly the aim was to encourage the thank offering to be shared widely, not hoarded. Perhaps there is also an allusion to the manna that God supplied day by day, teaching dependence on him.

FOR REFLECTION

What is our equivalent of spontaneous, freewill offerings expressing praise to God for his specific blessings? How about throwing a thanksgiving party?

WAVING & HEAVING

We are still dealing with peace offerings and suddenly come across words from two new roots. At least, we would in Hebrew (see the table on pp. 20–21). Unfortunately, English translations vary so much that it will be useful to give the literal translation found in the New King James Version:

[30] His own hands shall bring the offerings made by fire to the Lord. The fat with the breast he shall bring, that the breast may be **waved** as a **wave offering** before the Lord. [31] And the priest shall burn the fat on the altar, but the breast shall be Aaron's and his sons'. [32] Also the right thigh you shall give to the priest as a **heave offering** from the sacrifices of your peace offerings. [33] He among the sons of Aaron, who offers the blood of the peace offering, and the fat, shall have the right thigh for his part. [34] For the **breast of the wave offering** and the **thigh of the heave offering** I have taken from the children of Israel, from the sacrifices of their peace offerings, and I have given them to Aaron the priest and to his sons from the children of Israel by a statute forever.

The first root means 'to move to and fro, wave, sprinkle', hence the translation 'wave (offering)'. Most commentators assume that the movement was not from side to side but forwards and backwards, signifying offering. The NRSV and some commentators have 'elevation offering' but this does not seem justified.

The 'heave offering'—what a lovely term!—comes from the root 'to be lifted up, raised, exalted'. However, the word itself is usually reckoned to mean 'be lifted off, separated'—that is, 'from the common sphere into God's sphere'—and this seems to be appropriate where it occurs in the Old Testament. Recent translations assume the basic meanings 'contribution or offering'.

So the situation is this. We are dealing still with peace offerings or offerings of well-being. We have previously been told that the worshipper must offer the parts to be burnt (fat from various areas, 3:3–4; remember that the offering could be a cow or bull, sheep or goat). Now we find that the worshipper also brings the breast. The priests 'wave' it before the Lord but are allowed to keep it to eat. We are then told that the right thigh belongs to the priest who actually officiates at the sacrifice on behalf of the worshipper. The right thigh was one of the choicest parts then, as it is now. It was the portion that Saul received as the guest of honour in 1 Samuel 9:24.

Offered and shared with God

The significance of 'waving' is not explained. The common-sense conclusion might well be that it is a way of signifying that something is offered to God but still having it available for the priests to eat—just as we raise the collection plate after an offering is taken in church but still have the money to spend. Jewish commentators have elaborated in greater detail: the priest's portion is put upon the hands of the donor. The priest places his hands beneath those of the donor and moves them first forward and backward and then up and down, symbolizing consecration to God, the ruler of heaven and earth.

The most reliable way of working out the meaning of a word or phrase is to see how it is used. Perhaps the most interesting use of the term 'wave offering' is found in Numbers 8, where the whole tribe of Levi is said to be a 'wave offering from the Israelites before the Lord' (8:11). The reason given for the ritual is, 'for they are wholly given to [God]'.

Recap

Leviticus 7 ends with a brief summary (vv. 37–38), and it might be useful for us to survey what we have covered: burnt offerings (use still not made very clear), cereal offerings (basic use not yet clear, but could be an alternative sin offering for a poor person), peace offerings (various types: thanksgiving, vows and freewill offerings; wave offerings and heave offerings come in this category also), sin offerings (for different classes of people, to make atonement for sins committed unwittingly), and guilt offerings (similar to the sin offering but restitution is involved).

It is unlikely that ordinary people offered these sacrifices very regularly. Samuel's father went to the sanctuary once a year (1 Samuel 1:3), and he was a good and pious man. People were generally quite poor, so maybe the only time they ate meat was when they went to the sanctuary to offer peace offerings. These would be special times of rejoicing, times that those who live in the midst of plenty can scarcely appreciate.

MEDITATION

Meat—or another special treat—only once a year. Can you imagine (or remember) what it felt like?

DANGER: ORDINATION

Ordinands today are not issued with death threats at the start of their training, and in this they differ from the priests of Israel. The ominous warning in 8:35, 'keeping the Lord's charge so that you do not die' (compare also Exodus 30:20–21), will be seen to be justified in chapter 10, and the reader is alerted to the fact that these regulations must be taken with the utmost seriousness. They are not just 'nice ritual' but a test of obedience and aweful respect for God. More detailed instructions for the ordination or consecration of Aaron and his sons have already been given in Exodus 28—29; 30:22–30 (recipe and instructions for the anointing oil); and 40:12–15.

We have now seen the rituals for the various types of sacrifices and begin to find references to the situations in which each was used. Here we have an impressive number of animals for use in the ordination of Aaron and other priests:

- bull for a sin offering (vv. 2, 14–17)
- ram for a burnt offering (vv. 2, 18–21)
- ram for a wave offering, called the ordination offering (vv. 2, 22–29). (Remember that NRSV unhelpfully calls it an 'elevation offering'.)

The spectacle

The whole congregation gathered and waited at the entrance of the tent of meeting (the tabernacle), with Aaron and his 'sons' (that is, quite a number of descendants), dressed in linen garments, waiting for the vestments to be put on. Most people would not be able to see very well, if at all, and they would be told what was happening by words passed from person to person. Later on, most would have the chance to see the priests in their priestly garments and that visual evidence would be implanted firmly in their memories. The need for some 'sacramental' aspect to a ceremony seems to be strongly acknowledged in these accounts. The danger is simply that of thinking that ritual carried out carefully is sufficient in itself.

Moses begins the ceremony with the words, 'This is what the Lord has commanded to be done' (v. 5), then Aaron and his sons are washed with water. Common sense suggests that this is a sign of purity, which is confirmed by passages such as Numbers 19:11–22.

Aaron alone is clothed in tunic and sash, the robe, the ephod (with two shoulder-pieces, each containing a stone with the names of six of the tribes of Israel engraved on it), and the 'decorated band' or belt of the ephod. These are described in detail in Exodus 28, and were intended to be grand and impressive. They were made of gold, blue, purple and crimson.

The breastpiece (Exodus 28:15–34) is placed on Aaron with its twelve precious or semi-precious stones representing the twelve tribes of Israel. In the breastpiece also are placed the Urim and Thummim, used for receiving guidance from the Lord. We do not know exactly how these worked or what they looked like, but we can glean a little information from various references to them. For example, 1 Samuel 14:41–42 looks like a 'heads or tails' type of enquiry. On the other hand, it was possible to get a 'no reply' message, for in 1 Samuel 28:6 Saul could not get any guidance from God 'by dreams, or by Urim, or by prophets'. (See also the comment on Leviticus 5:14—6:7, p. 43.)

Splendour and simplicity

Today there is a strong difference of opinion between those who like to see Christian leaders officiating in highly decorative clothing, perhaps seen as pointing to the glory of God and the awesomeness of worship, and those who prefer 'ordinary' clothes, perhaps emphasizing the 'same-as-everyone-else' quality of the Christian minister. There is biblical warrant for both viewpoints and both seek to express aspects of the truth. Clearly the Old Testament rituals are of the former type.

The high priest of Israel had a rosette on his turban with the inscription 'Holy to the Lord' (Exodus 28:36), but Zechariah 14:20–21 looks forward to the time when even the bells on horses and cooking pots in the temple will have the inscription 'Holy to the Lord'. The prophecy surely has its fulfilment in us today, who have a greater privilege than the high priests of old to approach God directly at any time. I wonder if we also demonstrate in a visible way that we are holy to the Lord.

FOR REFLECTION

What do 'action rituals' add to a community's self-identity? What are the implications for things like marches for Jesus? Whitsunday processions? Downhill cheese rolling? Village fêtes?

ORDINATION (PART 2)

The first offering, as we read earlier in this chapter, was the burnt offering. We have seen the procedure before, but notice two things about this particular sacrifice: Moses is the officiating priest, and this is a one-off since he is installing the first high priest of Israel. Also see page xx–xx for comment on smearing blood on the altar and pouring blood at the base: it is 'to make atonement' for the altar. The verb used in verse ?? means 'to make (sacrifices) smoke' and seems to mean simply 'purify' or 'make fit for sacrificing'. Again this emphasizes the fact that God is so holy that nothing is automatically suitable for his service.

It must have taken some time for Moses to take the bull outside the camp and burn it there. We may imagine a crowd accompanying Moses (perhaps at a safe distance) as he moves some way away and burns the whole of the bull, apart from the fat and other parts that had been burnt on the altar. Normally the officiating priest would have received a portion of a sin offering (6:26, 29), but this one is actually offered for their consecration and so, presumably, that was not appropriate. Nevertheless, Moses receives part of the wave offering (v. 29, see below).

The bull and the two rams should be thought of as parts of one unified offering. The bull first prepares the place of sacrifice. Aaron and sons lay their hands on each of the rams, thus identifying with them. The burnt offering signifies (probably) the complete dedication of the priests to the Lord. The second ram, the ram of ordination, is eventually 'waved' (see comment on 7:28–38, pp. 48–49), but first some blood from the ram is put on Aaron's 'extremities'. The right earlobe, hand and big toe would serve as marking out the boundaries of the person as a whole and this *may* have been the symbolism. The ear features in Exodus 21:6 as a means of a slave's binding himself to his master for life. Perhaps a suggestive allusion was intended.

The anointed priests: Moses' successors

The choreography of the wave offering is interesting. Moses, as a sort of acting super-high priest, places the parts to be burnt on the hands of Aaron and his sons and himself guides their hands in the to-and-fro movement that the wave offering requires. This would presumably signify authorization of Aaron and his sons as priests from this point onwards, by Moses, God's specially appointed leader and mediator. We recall that it was Moses who received the call to act as the mediator between God and Pharaoh and between God and the Israelites. He it was who went up on to Mount Sinai to receive the law, and God spoke to him because the Israelites were afraid of having a direct communication from the Lord (Exodus 20:18–21; Deuteronomy 5:5; compare 18:16). Later on, God himself says that Moses is unlike anyone else because 'with him I speak face to face—clearly, not in riddles; and he beholds the form of the Lord' (Numbers 12:8). The basic function of the priest, especially the high priest, is to be a mediator between God and the people. Here Moses passes on that role to the tribe of Levi.

The recipe for anointing oil is given in Exodus 30:22–33. Clearly it was designed to make an impression upon the senses of the worshippers. So Aaron and his sons are anointed—set apart for God's service—in a memorable way, in fact in such a way that memories would in future be stimulated by the smell of that special anointing oil. Are there smells that remind you of particular experiences, commitments, and so on—smells that can assist you in 'the practice of the presence of God'? Some churches use incense, but perhaps there are other fragrances that might be helpful to worshippers.

The ordination retreat

Lastly (vv. 31–36), Aaron and his sons are confined to the entrance of the tent of meeting for seven days and seven nights. This would certainly mark out the ceremony as a particular weighty and significant one, and give space for those who had been ordained to meditate on the duties that lay ahead of them. Notice again the strict charge in verse 35. The chapter ends with the brief report that they did as the Lord commanded.

A priesthood was in place, pointing to and awaiting the time when Christ, the perfect high priest, would come.

FOR REFLECTION

Many times we have come across symbolism and ritual whose significance is unclear. How much does it matter? Are there resonances that cannot be put into words but which we nevertheless feel?

The NEW PRIESTS' FIRST DUTIES

Having spent seven days and nights confined to the entrance of the tent of meeting, Aaron and sons are now called upon to offer sacrifices. The requirements are extensive:

Aaron: Bull calf for a burnt offering (for Aaron himself, v. 8, but assisted by his sons).
Ram for a sin offering.

People: Male goat for a sin offering.
Calf and lamb (one year old) for a burnt offering.
Ox and ram for a peace offering (well-being): their breasts and right thighs as a wave offering.
Cereal offering (grain offering).

First Aaron offers the offerings, his own and those of the people. The burnt offerings and the sin offerings together are said to 'make atonement' for himself (and presumably his sons—or else they are included with 'the people') and for the people. Verses 8–21 describe Aaron's carrying out of the instructions, bringing the burnt offering 'piece by piece', which helps us a little as we try to imagine what the ceremony must have been like. Verse 21 also tells us that Aaron waved the breasts and right thigh of the peace offerings (ox and ram) as a wave offering. Hebrews 7:26–28 makes a contrast between these imperfect Levitical priests, Aaron and his descendants, and Christ, who had no need to offer a sin offering for himself.

Notice the motivation expressed in verse 6. The offerings are to be made so that 'the Lord may appear to you'. This is described at the end of the ceremony in verses 22–24: Aaron blesses the people and enters the tent of meeting with Moses, and 'the glory of the Lord appeared to all people' and 'fire came out from the Lord and consumed the burnt offering and the fat on the altar'. What are we to make of this? The fire has already been lit and sacrifices have been burnt. They would not have been completely burnt, since whole animals would take quite some time. So perhaps we are to imagine some sort of spectacular flare-up that finished off the procedure? Something remarkable is in view because the people 'saw it' and, in response, 'shouted and fell on their faces'. Probably a well-placed flash of lightning would have been quite effective!

Did it happen like that?

To many—probably most—people in the Western world, this account has an air of unreality about it. These things just don't happen in our experience, and many will find difficulty in accepting the text at face value. Others will find it easier to believe that God would show himself in a remarkable way—especially at this critical time in the history of God's people.

The passage teaches that God is a God of awesome power, holy and to be reverenced. He makes a difference in actual time and space—he is not a 'concept'. This passage must have had some influence on the way that 1 Kings 18 was understood. There, in the contest organized by Elijah between Yahweh (the Lord) and Baal, the latter is shown to be powerless or non-existent. Elijah mocks the prophets of Baal: 'Call out loudly. Perhaps he's meditating, or has wandered off somewhere... or possibly he's asleep and needs waking' (1 Kings 18:27). The Lord, on the other hand, sends down fire and burns up the wet sacrifice that Elijah has prepared (presumably with sea water?). Often in the Bible, fire is seen as something that purifies and/or judges (see Numbers 11:1–3; Deuteronomy 9:3; 32:22; 2 Kings 1:10–14; Amos 1:4—2:5, and many others), separating that which is worth saving from that which is dross (Isaiah 1:25). In the New Testament too, fire is found as a symbol of purifying: see, for example, 1 Peter 1:6–7. These references help us to understand the significance of events described in the Bible.

See also 1 Chronicles 21:26 at the end of the plague on the threshing floor of Ornan/Araunah.

FOR REFLECTION AND PRAISE

The glory of the Lord is seen in fire, smoke and bright lights, but 'glory' means essentially 'weight'. It expresses substance or worth and can be seen in unexpected places. 'The Word became flesh and dwelt among us, and we have seen his glory..., glory as of the only-begotten son of the Father, full of grace and truth'. 'When the centurion saw that in this way he breathed his last, he said, "Truly, this man was God's Son!"' (John 1:14; Mark 15:39).

15 LEVITICUS 10

STRANGE FIRE *before the* LORD

If the two people leading the service in your church on a Sunday morning were suddenly burnt up by fire, I wonder what your response would be. This is the situation described in Leviticus 10. Two of Aaron's four sons, Nadab and Abihu, went in for an unauthorized experiment and brought 'unholy fire before the Lord, such as he had not commanded them' (v. 1). There must have been great fear, if not panic. People would have been asking themselves and their neighbours, 'What happened? What does this mean? Are *we* in danger? Who is going to be able to explain this to us?' They would certainly never haave forgotten the event.

Actually it is not entirely clear where the event is placed, but probably inside the tent of meeting, so that the congregation are to be imagined seeing fire but not the deaths of the two radical liturgists. Nor are we told how Moses explained to them what had happened. Many things in the Bible are left to our imagination and/or common sense.

This God is love?

The passage presents an enormous challenge to us who believe that 'God is love' (1 John 4:8) and that he has 'no pleasure in the death of the wicked' (Ezekiel 33:11). Many reject either the passage or the whole of Christianity because the harshness of this punishment. In seeking to understand it, certain observations need to be made.

First, there are other similar events to be considered: the death penalty for the man gathering sticks on the sabbath (Numbers 15:32–36); the execution of Achan and his family for taking things that had been 'devoted to the Lord' and should have been destroyed (Joshua 7:1–2, 24–26); the commandments to 'utterly destroy' the Canaanites and also the Amalekites (see Deuteronomy 7:2; 1 Samuel 15:3). There is at least one similar event in the New Testament, the case of Ananias and Sapphira (Acts 5:1–11), and yet the Old Testament, as well as the New, asserts that God is 'merciful and gracious, slow to anger, and abounding in steadfast love and faithfulness' (for example, Exodus 34:6).

These harsh punishments occur at the beginning of a significant era in the history of God's people. Judgment does occur throughout the

Bible but it is nearly always after many warnings by prophets. Most of the time, Israel escaped deserved judgment for long periods. God is presented in both Old and New Testaments as severe in judgment but not arbitrary. His judgments have a determined educational purpose.

Lessons and ongoing struggle

This does not 'solve the problem' but it gives us guidelines for enlightened reflection. It is wrong to assert, as many have done, that this is an 'Old Testament problem' and the God of the New Testament is quite different. It is wrong to assert that God was 'always wiping people out in the Old Testament'. It is also wrong to make careless comparisons with modern examples of attempted genocide.

Some simply cannot accept in any sense that God actually did these things or commanded them. In that case, the text would simply be a way of teaching—as strongly as possible—the holiness and awesomeness of God, and the need to approach him with care and purity, and on his own terms. Some do accept that these things could have happened. In that case they will need to recognize that Israel was influenced by ideas that were current at the time (for example, it was accepted that people and families could be 'devoted to God' by being destroyed) and that God seems to work within the framework of understanding that people have.

Tough sympathy for Aaron

The sequel to the judgment is very hard for Aaron. He is not allowed to show signs of mourning (dishevelled hair and torn garments, v. 6) although the rest of the people are. No doubt this was to indicate acceptance of the justice of the Lord's action. He was to remain inside the tent and his cousins were to carry the bodies outside the camp.

Further instructions are given in verses 12–15 concerning the portions due to the priests. It is clear that there is sympathy for Aaron and his two remaining sons in their loss, and their failure to eat any of the sin offering allotted to them is not taken as a sign of neglect but understandable sorrow—and loss of appetite? The regular expected procedures are made clear (v. 17).

FOR REFLECTION AND PRAYER

O Lord, in wrath may you remember mercy.

Habakkuk 3:2

CLEAN & UNCLEAN CREATURES

The principle for deciding which land animals are clean is first given (vv. 1–8). They must:

- have divided hoofs. This rules out camel, rock badger and hare.
- be cleft-footed. Some translations include this in with the 'divided hoofs' category, but 11:26 implies that an animal may have divided hoofs without being cleft-footed. Apparently the camel's hoof is split on the top but not underneath (Rabbi Rashi, c. 1040).
- chew the cud. This rules out the pig.

Kosher: an opportunity for obedience

It has frequently been noted that it is wise not to eat pork in certain regions, especially hot ones, since the meat goes off quickly, and pigs' undiscerning palate makes them liable to pick up and pass on parasites and the like. This would provide a good reason for God to ban it, but it is not the reason given. So what was in God's mind, we do not know. We do know that the Israelites were *strictly* forbidden to eat certain meats, and the issue is fundamentally obedience to God's requirements. In other spheres, even today, it has been noted that carelessness with respect to 'the Maker's instructions' can lead to all sorts of physical problems. I wonder if tobacco would have been banned, had the practice of smoking been known then.

Jewish kosher laws today rule out these animals. In Western countries, there is not much temptation to eat camels or rock badgers, and even jugged hare has limited appeal. Pork (including bacon) is avoided by all but the most liberal Jews.

Another less likely suggested reason is that to be clean, an animal in any category must belong purely to that category, and not have characteristics that are 'mixed'. This makes sense in the light of Genesis 1:24 ('everything according to its kind') and certain laws against mixing—different kinds of seed, different clothing materials and different animals yoked together for ploughing (Deuteronomy 22:9–11). This idea does not work for the other categories of creatures, however, and remains a guess.

Creatures of water and air

In the case of water creatures (vv. 9–12), those that are edible must have fins and scales. This rules out all reptiles and also shellfish, including lobster and crab, as well as shrimps, prawns, mussels and eels, which have fins but not scales. In 11:29–30, examples are given of some creatures related to these (lizards and so on), with a few additions—weasel, mouse and chameleon.

There are no principles stated for forbidden birds, but a list is given (vv. 13–19). Deuteronomy 14:11 says, 'You may eat any clean birds' but does not specify any either. We know at least that pigeons, turtle doves (Leviticus 1:14–17) and quails (Exodus 16:11–13; Numbers 11:31–33) were acceptable—unless you only got the quails by grumbling. Unfortunately, we are not sure of the identification of some of these birds and Bible translations differ in their guesses. Several of them might be thought undesirable because they eat the flesh of animals that have died or been killed and left, that are often well beyond their use-by date. We can note also that we would not include the bat as a bird but a mammal. The Hebrew word translated 'bird' means 'winged creature' and does not intend to offer any sort of zoological classification.

Winged insects are next (vv. 20–23). All that walk on 'four feet' (sic) are forbidden, except those with jointed legs with which they leap—locusts and grasshoppers. We know that John the Baptist lived on locusts and wild honey out in the desert. It must have been quite a hard existence, since locusts are worse than buses—too few or far too many—and honey is not normally plentiful. No doubt 'the Lord provided' and John learnt a lesson similar to that of the Israelites with manna in the desert (Deuteronomy 8:2–3; Matthew 4:2–4).

Perhaps the most significant clue we have concerning the significance of the food laws comes from Acts 10. In a vision, Peter is commanded to eat various unclean animals. When he objects to this, a voice says, 'What God has made clean, you must not call profane.' The meaning of this is that the Gentiles have now been 'cleansed': they can now become God's people through the sacrifice of Christ.

FOR REFLECTION

*Eating pork is a sacrament too. Once forbidden, unclean;
now clean, permitted—and delicious. May it remind us that we
Gentiles who were far off are now admitted to God's table.*

17 LEVITICUS 11:24–47

UNCLEANNESS: TRANSMISSION,
PREVENTION & CURE

In Mark 7, Jesus tells the disciples that it is not what goes into the body that defiles (food) but what comes out (bad words). We have accounts of Jesus deliberately touching lepers, who were the unclean of the unclean. We also know of the importance of touch for those who feel themselves to be outcasts. An illustration of this in recent times was Princess Diana's willingness to touch hospital patients who had AIDS—without the use of the traditional 'royal gloves'—and we know how much this was appreciated. So it is particularly difficult to think ourselves back into the world of ritual uncleanness.

The laws governing uncleanness were there as an educational tool, a 'schoolteacher' as Paul might have put it (compare Galatians 3:24). They demonstrate and make concrete the fact that God is pure and holy, that those who approach him must also be pure, and that defilement can be communicated from one person to another. Bad company ruins good morals (1 Corinthians 15:33).

So the chapter continues with teaching on uncleanness. Previously the focus has been on eating; now it is on touching, but the two groups of creatures mentioned seem to be the same. Both groups are described as 'unclean' and there is considerable overlap. Uncleanness, therefore, is contracted by touching *carcasses of unclean creatures* (v. 24) and those who do must wash their clothes and remain unclean until the evening. The ritual nature of the requirement is made clear, since no physical cleansing actually takes place between the washing and the evening.

The same regulation is given for further classes and examples of unclean creatures and objects:

- Animals that have paws (the Hebrew literally means 'palms'), such as the cat and dog families (vv. 26–27). This has been explained as a perversion of what is normal—walking on 'hands'. Others simply take the word to mean 'pads' and sometimes also regard these animals as unclean because they are carnivores.

- Swarming creatures (vv. 29–30; see comment on vv. 20–23,

p. 59). There is a further emphatic warning against these in verses 41–45, where they are described as not just unclean but 'detestable'. Implied here but previously unmentioned are snakes and centipedes. Verses 44–45 give special force to Ezekiel's vision of creeping things and loathsome animals in the temple (Ezekiel 8:9–10).

- Any article used for human purposes which comes into contact with unclean creatures (v. 32). Most of these things can be washed and become clean in the evening, with the following exceptions. An earthenware vessel must be broken—perhaps because it is porous and cannot be properly cleansed. This is not entirely certain, however, because the word used is 'clay vessel' and the use of glaze was normal. In that case it may be that clay vessels were more associated with food ready for eating. In any case, they were cheap and the symbolism was not too expensive! Water that becomes contaminated is a dangerous means of spreading the problem (v. 34)—as we know very well. Ovens and stoves (v. 35) would also be made of clay and would be easily replaced.

- Clean animals that simply die—that is, are not ritually (or deliberately?) slaughtered (vv. 39–40).

Causing or signifying uncleanness

Two important exceptions are given in verses 36–38. It is obviously vital to know where the boundaries of uncleanness are, and there is a clear difference between those things that cause uncleanness (creatures and water), and those that are temporarily unclean but savable. The supply of water and seeds needs to be protected, since both are crucial for the very survival of the people. Consequently, even if an unclean creature falls into a storage cistern, the water and the cistern remain clean. Similarly, seed intended for sowing is clean and should not be destroyed. Verse 38 is unclear but probably means seed intended for eating: possibly seed being soaked for this purpose is in mind.

REFLECTION

Was the food that Elijah got from the ravens unclean? (1 Kings 17:4–6). If so, is this a precursor of Acts 10:15?

NEITHER MALE NOR FEMALE?
SPOT *the* DIFFERENCE

This chapter is one that many women have objected to very strongly and many men have felt embarrassed about. It is easy to see why. The subject is uncleanness after birth.

- For a baby boy, the mother is ceremonially unclean for seven days. A purification period of 33 days is prescribed (presumably in addition, bringing the number to the round and special number, 40). The baby is circumcised on the eighth day.

- For a baby girl, the mother is ceremonially unclean for fourteen days. A (further) purification period of 66 days is prescribed.

Learning from the regulations

What is the reason for this discrepancy and does it warrant criticism or rejection of Old Testament teaching? Many have thought so. The issue is not easily settled, not only because of a lack of reliable information, but because many have been hurt by the actions of those who have used such texts to justify their own discriminatory practices. It is therefore difficult to judge with a clear mind and heart. Some points may be made.

As we see in many places in the Old Testament (and even the New) God works with people from where they are. For example, sacrifice is a temporary measure; 'putting to the ban' is allowed; slavery continues in the Church for centuries and God does not overrule our blindness in this matter. 'God has overlooked times of human ignorance...' (Acts 17:30). It is therefore difficult to predict what aspects of a patriarchal society God will go along with and what he will change. It is not necessarily a lack of regard for the scriptures to accept that certain provisions of the law were imperfect (recall Mark 7:18–19; John 8:4–7, 11).

The belief of the times was that certain bodily actions were defiling in some way. These included childbirth, monthly periods, bodily discharges (male and female) and excretion, and certain types of illness. Incidentally, in some Christian cultures the monthly period is regarded as defiling. Sex is not regarded as unclean in biblical thought, despite the fact that this idea has been promoted by certain Christian communities and churches over the centuries. Still less is childbirth a bad thing in any way: it is a huge blessing (especially when it's over!).

The point has been made before that these ritual requirements are visual aids (recall that blood would be eaten in meat, since not all can be removed, however the animal is killed and treated). These regulations point to the awesome nature of giving birth. It is a miracle of God who gives life to all.

Why the difference?

We are left no further towards knowing the reason for the double length of purification for a baby girl—if, indeed, there is a reason. Apparently, experiments were done, early in the 20th century, which showed a *slightly* longer time of recovery from the birth of a girl. Some ancient writers thought that there was greater danger in bearing a female child—some said there was greater danger from demons. Some have thought that the male child's circumcision contributes somehow to the purification. A more 'theological' explanation considers Genesis 2:16–17 and 3:15 together, concluding that 'in giving birth, the woman challenges the penalty of death on humanity for sin... Each birth strikes a blow on the head of the serpent' (Hartley, p. 169). I am still left with the suspicion that this law arose from primitive prejudices that God went along with for the time being.

Jesus' parents brought him to the temple in order to fulfil these regulations (Luke 2:22–24; note the evidence here that Joseph and Mary were poor—unable to afford a lamb), emphasizing that Jesus was 'born under the law' (Galatians 4:4; compare Matthew 3:14–15). While there, they received the bonus of the prophecies of Simeon and Anna (Luke 2:29–35, 38).

FOR FURTHER THOUGHT

Many people today live under imperfect laws, or under law enforced by prejudiced people. Are there principles to guide them in their attitudes and action?

DEALING *with* 'LEPROSY'

The malignant skin disease translated 'leprosy', here and in other places in the Bible, is not identical with (but might possibly include) what we call leprosy today, that is, Hansen's disease. At least some of the symptoms described are quite different, and the term is a broad one for it includes moulds, mildews and mineral efflorescence in walls or fabrics.

In Leviticus 13, various cases of symptoms that resemble leprosy are considered. A *possible* identification with a modern disease is given in various commentaries and books (especially R.K. Harrison; see the bibliography). Some scholars think that *some* of the cases below describe Hansen's disease, but most scholars would not equate any of the Leviticus 13 descriptions with clinical (modern) leprosy.

Symptoms and diagnosis

Verses 2–8:   Swelling, eruption/scab or spot/shiny patch—with white hair. Harrison thinks that this might be Hansen's disease.

Verses 9–17:   White swelling or ulcerating tissue in the skin. 'Raw flesh' is the worrying sign here.

Verses 18–23: Change in a healed boil.

Verses 24–28: Reddish-white or white spot after a burn.

Verses 29–37: Itching disease in the hair or beard.

Verses 38–39: Dull white spots on the body.

Verses 40–44: Baldness. Verse 40 is very reassuring to many men: if anyone loses the hair from his head, he is bald—but he is clean.

Verses 45–46: Regulations for all lepers—appearance, words, dwelling.

Verses 47–58: Disease in clothing.

Basic principles

Verses 2–8 give us the basic plan for dealing with worrying symptoms. The three words together (swelling, eruption, spot) are probably intended to include all sorts of conditions of the skin—pimples, blisters, boils, tumours, scabs, dandruff, sores and so on. These sensible procedures recommend *examination*, *precautions* and *observation*. The first case is of a spot, swelling or eruption that has not healed up. If there is hair in it that has turned white and it seems to be deeper than the skin, then the priest is to pronounce the sufferer unclean.

The priest acts as a sort of 'barefoot doctor', such as are known in many countries where professional health care is inaccessible because of distance or finance. He requires an elementary knowledge of the symptoms of different kinds of skin and/or hair problem. The fact that the law required the priestly examination would have gone some way to overcoming the reluctance that patients (ancient or modern) have in admitting their symptoms—even to themselves. The priest might make three kinds of judgment: 'not leprous and clean' (vv. 38–40); 'leprous and therefore unclean' (v. 3); or 'isolation pending further examinations' (after seven and fourteen days), after which a 'clean or unclean' decision must be declared (vv. 4–8). The regulations have important health implications, as is seen in the isolation of the leper and the requirement that they warn people of their condition (vv. 45–46). Nevertheless, the main focus is on ritual cleanness or uncleanness—fitness to come into the presence of the Lord.

Sickness and isolation

Those with leprosy must have provided a powerful visual aid for other Israelites, but the cost they themselves bore was enormous. In former times, to contract leprosy was normally to receive the death sentence. The torn clothes, unkempt hair, and covering of the lower part of the face are all common signs of mourning. They were effectively cut off from the people for ever. The New Testament indicates that the Lord's real attitude towards those who have such diseases is compassion. So we read in Matthew 8:3 that Jesus stretched out his hand and *touched* the leper who came to him and said, 'I do choose [to make you clean]. Be clean.' It is interesting that the leper asked to be made clean rather than to be healed, and this is the common expression concerning leprosy in the New Testament. To be accepted is more important than to be physically healthy.

FOR REFLECTION

What restrictions or freedom do these regulations imply for additional (e.g. scientific) methods of diagnosis and treatment of illnesses? If the Law had been given today, would priests have been supplied with microscopes? Or would the sufferer have been required to bring a medical certificate to the priest?

'LEPROSY' IN PEOPLE & HOUSES

Chapter 13 dealt with diagnosis and response to various skin complaints. Chapter 14:1–32 deals with purification after recovery from the disease. A summary may again be helpful.

Procedures

The priest (vv. 2b–3a) goes out of the camp, where the leper had to be living, and the leper is brought to him. The order is confusing but Hebrew tenses do not emphasize the sequence as English normally does.

The priest (vv. 4–7) slaughters one (clean) bird over fresh water in an earthenware vessel, dips four items in its blood (a living bird, cedarwood, hyssop and crimson yarn—probably used to tie the items together to make a sort of mop-sprinkler), sprinkles the blood seven times on the one to be cleansed and pronounces him clean, and releases the living bird into the air (carrying blood from the sacrificed bird). This sending up into the air is similar to the *Yom Kippur* sending away of the goat into the desert.

The one to be cleansed (vv. 8–10) washes his clothes, shaves completely, and washes himself. He lives inside the camp but outside his tent for seven days, washes as before (head, beard and eyebrows are singled out for special mention), and (on the eighth day) brings two male lambs and one ewe lamb to the priest.

The priest (vv. 11–20) offers one lamb as a reparation offering/wave offering (see comment on 5:14–26, pp. 42–43; NRSV is inconsistent in translating 'elevation offering' here and in vv. 21 and 24), and puts some of its blood on the right ear lobe, right thumb and right big toe of the one to be cleansed. He sprinkles oil before the Lord seven times and puts some of the remainder on the worshipper in the same places as the blood, and pours the rest of the oil on the worshipper's head.

Then *the priest* offers the other two lambs (or two birds, if the leper is poor, vv. 21–31) as a sin offering and a burnt offering, together with a grain (cereal) offering. Thus the priest makes atonement for the cleansed person. All the main types of sacrifice are included here except for the peace offering, which was almost always voluntary. Why the reparation offering? Possibly because of doubt concerning whether the worshipper had committed some sin, or possibly to compensate God for the offerings which could not be made during the person's time of uncleanness (Wenham, p. 210).

The procedures for dealing with houses affected by disease that might or might not spread is similar. That which is likely to spread is removed outside the camp—possibly the plaster from the walls, or even the stones themselves.

The leper's lot

As hinted at in the previous reading, the lot of the leper must have been particularly dreadful in those times. In addition to the symptoms of the disease, they would have had to leave their closest family—no more hugs from children or parents. They had no access to the normal life of the people but were compelled to live outside the camp. If others came near, they were to call out '[I am] unclean', warning that they had a contagious condition. They would be deprived of the protection provided by a group of people living together. They would be despised and shunned, possibly mocked and looked down upon. The book of Job, although set outside Israel, gives a picture of life on the rubbish dump—made worse by the memory of what had been previously (Job 30:9–15; cf. Job 29).

Most people in the Western world have no first-hand experience of the sort of skin diseases signified in these Old Testament texts. Hansen's disease is known in many parts of the world, and those who work among lepers know how important it is for them to be accepted by their fellow human beings. Most people are still hesitant to touch them even when it is known that the disease has passed its contagious phase. The 'right hand of fellowship' has extra significance for such sufferers.

In view of this, it was particularly important to have a strong and visible ritual to mark recovery from the disease. Several features of it are obscure but the overall impact is clear. It would be like a sacrament signifying to healed persons and all their neighbours that they truly had been healed and restored to fellowship with God. There was, therefore, no excuse for anyone to refuse to associate with them.

FOR REFLECTION

How can society be organized so that the healthy touching that is so necessary to human well-being is not unnecessarily inhibited or misinterpreted, but abuse is prevented?

21   LEVITICUS 15 (i)

BODILY DISCHARGES

I wondered if I should give a warning—'If you are squeamish, move on to chapter 16'—but probably the title is enough. However, the medical feel of parts of this chapter again remind us that the whole of life comes under God's oversight and within his concern, and this includes both the runny and the gooey which causes blockages (v. 3).

The structure of this chapter is chiastic and looks like this:

a Abnormal male discharges (vv. 2–15)
  b Normal male discharges and sexual intercourse (vv. 16–18)
  b Normal female discharges and sexual intercourse (vv. 19–24)
a Abnormal female discharges (vv. 25–30)

Common principles

Old Testament rules are quite often sacramental. In other words, a physical phenomenon has a spiritual significance. The first twelve verses of this chapter almost read like a (very sensible) health manual dealing with a contagious disease. The infection may be passed on directly (vv. 7–8, 10: by bodily contact, spittle, or unwashed hands) or indirectly (vv. 4–6, 9–10: via bed, seat or saddle). The remedy is washing and staying away from contact with others until the evening. All earthenware vessels that have become infected are to be broken (presumably because they cannot be adequately sterilized) but wooden vessels are to be washed with water. These simple rules, and similar ones, have been introduced into many communities and have saved many lives.

They raise the question of what should be done when a people discovers, through experiment (science) or other means, that water washing is not enough in many cases. Do they incorporate new and more exacting procedures into the 'divine' law? Do they simply add 'human' rules and regard them as less important? Do they understand the law as figurative and implying the further discoveries that they have made? There is a strong case to be made for seeing principles laid down as required by God. In other words, the law says something like: 'You shall take all possible measures to avoid the spread of infection.' It is

easily seen that this follows also from the second great commandment, 'You shall love your neighbour as yourself.'

Nasty or natural

Some unpleasant features of a person are displeasing to God and
some are merely natural (see Mark 7), but physical blemishes all
have the possibility of communicating a message about evil. Physical
uncleanness is a sign of spiritual uncleanness, that is, unfitness to
be in God's presence (compare also Isaiah 6:5; Luke 5:8). This idea
can also be abused and, when made into a hard and absolute rule,
it has to be rejected (Mark 7:14–23). But its powerful educational
message is that uncleanness defiles and its effects can spread unless
careful measures are taken to counteract them. The sacrifices prescribed (vv. 14–15, 29) are an important witness to the fact of
healing, the obedience of the worshipper, and a public demonstration of the fact that the formerly unclean person is now reincorpo-
rated into the people of God. The sacrifices also have a positive value
in implying what need not be done: the person may continue to live
at home and is not required to live in isolation, as with leprosy.
There is therefore no justification for others to treat them in a worse
manner.

Note that Leviticus 20:18 requires a severe penalty for sexual
intercourse during menstruation—which may suggest that chapter
15 refers only to unwitting intercourse or, less likely, contact without
intercourse (see comment on Leviticus 20, pp. 86–87).

FOR REFLECTION

*How is it that so many apparent opposites seem to be separated
only by a thin wall? Genius and madness? Love and hate—or
infatuation and loathing? The sacred and the defiled? Do you
know of a good health and safety policy?*

MALE & FEMALE DISCHARGES

In the previous reading we looked at common principles in dealing with male and female bodily discharges. Today we look at some of the differences.

Specifics and differences

Since verses 16–17 speak of a one-off emission of semen, it seems clear that verses 1–12 deal with abnormal emissions from the penis. The word used is literally 'flesh', which has a variety of derived meanings, but which is clearly used to mean 'vagina' in verse 19. These emissions require washing and a period of ritual uncleanness but no sacrifices. Note that those who were to perform holy acts, including war, were obliged to refrain from sexual intercourse beforehand (compare 1 Samuel 21:4–5; 2 Samuel 11:11: Uriah refused to go and lie with his wife while the army was out in the field, even when David got him drunk).

Comment has been made on the difference, even 'unfairness', of the fact that a man is only unclean until the evening and a woman for seven days. Responses offered include the fact that the monthly period is a bigger deal than an ejaculation and needs to be marked more clearly. It lasts longer, it is more problematic physically, and it is of much greater significance with respect to conception.

Many would also say that there *was* discrimination in favour of men and against women in biblical times, and that this is simply an example of it (see comment on Leviticus 12, pp. 62–63). It seems clear also, however, that both in the Bible and in more recent experience, God educated his people slowly, starting from the widely accepted beliefs that they already held.

Minor problems and husbands

Verses 16–17 deal with an emission of (normal) semen which seems to be apart from sexual intercourse. No sacrifice is required (perhaps reassuring to boys who have recently reached puberty?) but both the person and any object on which semen falls are to be washed and remain unclean until the evening.

Within marriage, the instructions here would serve to make husbands aware of the fact that God is always present. Sexual intercourse is intended for pleasure but not one-sided pleasure or exploitation. Women's natural rhythms are to be respected. Consideration and self-discipline are commanded within a relationship where familiarity can become contempt, or other unloving attitudes.

Many have concluded from this chapter that there is something dirty about sex, or else that the Bible *regards* sex as dirty and therefore has an unhealthy attitude towards it. This is to misunderstand the chapter: sexual intercourse is not dirty, but it is dangerous, because it is sacred. At the beginning of the Old Testament, God commands human beings to 'be fruitful and multiply': sex is a gift from God to be used in the way that he instructs. A wife is a great blessing (a 'good thing', in the words of Proverbs 18:22) and young men are instructed to 'rejoice in the wife of your youth' (Proverbs 5:18).

FOR FURTHER THOUGHT

What must the woman have felt who had a haemorrhage and furtively touched Jesus in the crowd? How relieved when, far from rebuking her, he healed her and commended her faith! Have we faith to show the same sort of cheeky expectation?

The DAY *of* ATONEMENT (i)

Here we approach the most holy place in Israelite religion. *Yom Kippur,* or the 'Day of Atonement', is central to Jewish faith and practice today and crucial for Christian theology. Once a year, the high priest was allowed to go inside the holy of holies (the 'most holy place') within the tabernacle (or, after Solomon's time, the temple) to present the blood of sacrifice on behalf of the whole people. For anyone else to enter 'behind the curtain', or even for the high priest to enter at the wrong time or without careful observance of the regulations, was to court extreme danger (v. 2). Note how the opening of the chapter (v. 1) refers to the death of Aaron's sons, Nadab and Abihu, a particularly horrifying visual aid in teaching the holiness of God (Leviticus 10). We shall return to this below.

Outline of the ritual

The ceremony itself consisted of the following elements.

* Aaron washes and then puts on linen undergarments, tunic, sash and turban (v. 4).

* He brings his own bull and ram, plus a ram and two goats taken from the people (vv. 3, 5).

* He enters the 'holy place' (the section outside the 'holy of holies') and offers a young bull for a sin offering for himself and his household (vv. 6, 11–14; see below).

* Aaron takes two goats to the door of the tent of meeting (later, temple) and casts lots on them (vv. 7–8).

* One is to be presented to the Lord as a sin offering. The other is to be sent off into the desert 'for Azazel' (traditional translation, 'as a scapegoat') (vv. 8–10).

* Aaron offers a burnt offering for himself and the people—presumably two rams (vv. 24, 3, 5).

Overall significance

Several features of the Day of Atonement stand out prominently. It is emphasized several times that *permission to approach God is not a natural right but a great and dangerous privilege*. Aaron's sons have just died because they offered 'strange fire' (see ch. 10) before the Lord—incense that had not been authorized. The high priest is warned that, in order to survive his entry into the holy of holies, Aaron must come at the appointed time (v. 2) and put incense on the fire so that the cloud covers the mercy seat (v. 13). (See also Leviticus 10:6–8.)

The detailed regulations, including the emphasis on washing and a complete 'holy outfit', confirm that careful obedience is vitally important. The ritual must be done every year: the idea of a once-for-all sacrifice has not yet been envisaged. The high priest is not actually fit to come before God on behalf of the people and must be granted access by God's grace. The bull offered as a sin offering would serve to give both teaching and assurance. Actions often speak deeper than words.

As Christians we are privileged to 'enter the holy of holies' through the sacrifice of Christ. The tearing of the veil in the temple, reported by Matthew, Mark and Luke (27:51; 15:38 and 23:45 respectively) is meant to signify this fact. The writer to the Hebrews develops this theme in speaking of a heavenly sanctuary, into which Jesus has entered (Hebrews 6:19; 9:3; 10:20). The teaching of both Old and New Testaments is completely in harmony here. The salvation we have through Christ was hard won: we are 'ransomed... not with perishable things like silver and gold but with the precious blood of Christ, like that of a lamb without defect or blemish (1 Peter 1:18–19; compare 1 Corinthians 6:20; 7:23). Yet, it is very difficult to avoid taking things for granted—even this. In normal life, little faults are so *normal*, even endearing. The Old Testament does not have the full revelation of Christ that is given in the New, but it still has a vital role in making us aware of the absolute necessity of coming before God in complete purity. The only way is through the sacrifice of Christ, prefigured many centuries before his birth and part of God's unchanging policy on sin.

FOR MEDITATION

'Just as I am, without one plea but that thy blood was shed for me.' Do you find that to be true? Or do you plead other things, for example, your own comparative goodness? Does Leviticus 16 help?

The DAY of ATONEMENT (ii)

The well-known Hebrew phrase used by Jews today, *Yom Kippur*, is not found in the Hebrew Bible. What we do find is *yom hakkippurim* which means literally 'the day of coverings or atonements', the plural probably signifying a superlative—a day of full and complete atonement. It is found in Leviticus 23:27 and 25:9 (compare 'a day of atonement' in 23:28) and the term for the 'mercy seat' is derived from the same verb. Chapter 16:30 gives us the best summary of the whole ritual: 'atonement shall be made for you, to cleanse you; from all your sins you shall be clean before the Lord'. Scholars think it unlikely that the term carried any of the original meaning of 'covering up, covering over' (which could be used for hush-money, as in 1 Samuel 12:3): it had become a technical term.

Today, religious Jews take *Yom Kippur* very seriously. They fast from one evening to the next and much of that time of fasting is spent in prayer and worship. An important expectation of this high holy day is mutual forgiveness. In Israel it is very quiet on this day since virtually all refrain from work (v. 29), and that was the reason why the Arab nations bordering Israel chose *Yom Kippur* (6 October) as the day to attack Israel in 1973. The end of the fast is a time of rejoicing together.

Incense and blood within the veil

Aaron's brief is to take a censer with fire from the altar, put incense upon it and bring it inside the holy of holies. The incense cloud is to cover the 'mercy seat' (*kapporeth*), which was a slab of gold, about 140cm by 60cm, covering the 'ark of the testimony/covenant' (v. 2). On top of this were two cherubim, with wings touching each other, thus making a throne for the Lord. This is the place where atonement is made: Aaron takes blood from the bull and sprinkles it on and in front of the mercy seat. The number seven probably indicates 'completeness' here (v. 14) and often elsewhere. Having done that for his own sins, and those of his household, he brings the blood of the people's sin-offering goat and does the same (vv. 15–16). It is reckoned that he makes atonement not only for the people but also for the sanctuary and the tent of meeting. Remember that there are basically three areas—the outer one where the altar for sacrifice stood, the 'holy place' where the incense altar was and where the priests went each day, and the 'most holy place' or 'holy of holies' where only the high priest went, and only once a year.

Azazel or the scapegoat

It came as a shock, many years ago, to find that the familiar 'scape-goat', the means of passing your sins on to another, had been re-placed in new translations by the mystifying expression 'Azazel'. The word occurs only in this chapter of the Bible. It may be the name of a spirit haunting desert regions, but the meaning seems to be 'entire removal'. It is unlikely that the Israelites thought of an actual demon receiving the goat in the desert, though perhaps that was the origin of the word. After all, we use the words 'tantalizing' and 'titanic' with-out thinking that this implies belief in the real existence of the god Tantalus or the Titans of Greek mythology. The meaning here must be discerned from the context, and clearly the goat 'takes away the sins of the people' into the desert. Verse 21 is the most explicit: 'confess over it all the iniquities of the people of Israel... putting them on the head of the goat, and sending it away into the wilderness'. The fact that this goat is mentioned along with the goat for a sin offering sug-gests that together they make up one message—that sin is removed and destroyed.

Notice the emphasis throughout on washing, for transitions in both directions between the world of human beings and the heavenly realms.

QUESTIONS

What can we learn from the Old Testament and from Jewish friends today about approaching God in the way that pleases him? How do the two goats complement each other? Do they demand a unified interpretation?

The HOLINESS CODE

Chapters 18—26 frequently mention the need for holiness, hence the above name given by scholars. Leviticus 17 links the first part of the book, which deals largely with regulations for public life and worship, and the second part, which goes on to more personal concerns.

Slaughter regulations

It looks as though every animal that was killed in Israel had to be offered as a sacrifice, and the penalty for failing in this was to be banished (vv. 3–4). That seems rather harsh, to say the least. So what actually is this chapter saying?

The main concern is to avoid falling into idolatry or, rather, to change the practices of some Israelites who were already apparently involved in offering sacrifices to 'goat demons' (v. 7).

This suggests that what is regulated is not absolutely all killing of animals, but animals for sacrifice. Indeed, the word used for slaughter in verse 3 most frequently refers to slaughter for sacrifice. The chapter is therefore emphasizing the fact that sacrifices need to be offered to the Lord and in the Lord's own way. Verses 8 and 9 confirm this and extend the regulation to resident aliens. Similarly, verse 13 envisages the case of hunting for food and merely gives the command that the blood should be poured out and covered with earth.

No exemptions for aliens?

Verses 8, 12 and 15 expect resident aliens to conform to these religious laws. To what extent now should nations regulate religious practices within their own country? Christians are concerned—rightly, we believe—about the persecution of Christians and other groups in other countries. At the time of writing, many countries do not allow groups to gather for worship unless they belong to a particular religion or sub-group within a religion, or unless they have legally registered, or unless they fulfil other restrictions. The vast majority of countries, however, agree in principle to freedom of conscience—and also that certain freedoms need to be controlled. Does the passage offer any guidelines for our own very different situation?

Non-Jews can eat kosher food and non-Muslims can eat halal. Anyone can manage without pork, if necessary. So it is sometimes easy for people with differing convictions to accommodate to each other. Problems arise when what I feel I must do offends or causes problems for others.

The life is in the blood

Verses 10–16 have been discussed exhaustively by scholars. Some have thought that, to the ancient Israelites, blood had some sort of mystic quality, perhaps some sort of life force. Others have argued that the blood poured out implies the ending of life, the giving up of one life as a substitute for another.

The actual regulations set out here give us the best guidance. People must not eat blood, so it is not simply a form of life that can be eaten to strengthen the eater. It belongs to God and God has given it for a particular, important purpose—to make atonement (v. 11). One clear message, therefore, is that life is sacred to God. We have noted previously that it is not possible to drain every drop of blood from an animal, and the purpose of the regulation is symbolic and sacramental rather than physical or magical. In other words, these actions are commanded, and in doing them the people were supposed to give attention to their meaning. Jewish friends tell me that the kosher laws can be a powerful reminder to them of God's governance of the whole of life.

The last verses (vv. 15–16) deal with the case of animals that are not slaughtered but either die (from disease or old age) or are killed by wild animals. Nomads can't be choosers, most of the time. The penalty for eating is not banishment but simply washing as for other forms of minor uncleanness.

FOR MEDITATION

'Drink this in remembrance that Christ died for you.' Are there actions or visual aids in everyday life that remind you—or could remind you—of the presence of God?

The FORBIDDEN DEGREES

The structure of this chapter is very clear.

Vv. 1–5:   A new introductory section with an emphatic exhortation to keep God's statutes, *by doing which, one shall live.*

Vv. 6–16:   Sexual intercourse forbidden with near (up to two steps removed) relatives: father (v. 7), mother (v. 8), sister or half-sister (v. 9), granddaughter (v. 10), step-sister (v. 11), aunt (vv. 12–13), including aunt by marriage (v. 14), daughter-in-law (v. 15), sister-in-law (v. 16).

Vv. 17–18:   Also forbidden is intercourse with a woman *and* her daughter or granddaughter (v. 17) or sister (v. 18).

Vv. 19–23:   Various prohibitions: intercourse during a monthly period (v. 19); adultery with a neighbour's wife (v. 20); sacrificing your children to Molech (v. 21); homosexual activity (v. 22); bestiality (v. 23; see comment on ch. 20, pp. 86–87).

Vv. 24–30:   Stern closing exhortations. 'Do not commit any of these abominations as the Canaanites do: I am Yahweh your God.' Israel must be different—holy to Yahweh.

The opening verses suggest that this section might have stood on its own at one time, and it introduces a series of chapters that constantly repeat the need to be holy—for 'the Lord your God is holy'.

I am Yahweh: be holy

The brief formula in verse 30 and elsewhere reminds hearers of the amazing and gracious intention of God in making a covenant with Abraham and his descendants: 'I will be your God and you shall be my people.' 'I am Yahweh (the Lord)'—remember what this name signifies (compare Exodus 3:13–15; 6:2–8); 'I am *your* God'—remember the privileges and responsibilities that go with this.

Verse 5 is picked up by the apostle Paul as indicating the basis for 'justification through the law' (Romans 10:5; Galatians 3:12): in order to be acceptable to God through the law, you must keep all of it per-fectly. However, Paul's interpretation is an extension of the original emphasis: in keeping God's laws (within a covenant relationship) there is life—and, we might add, joy and fulfilment.

Out-of-bounds sex

Verse 6 contains two Hebrew euphemisms: 'draw near' can be used on its own to indicate sexual intercourse (Isaiah 8:3: 'I drew near to the prophetess, and she conceived and bore a son'; also Leviticus 18:14, 19; 20:16; Genesis 20:4; Ezekiel 18:6). The expression 'uncover the naked-ness/genitals' is also used on its own in this chapter and elsewhere.

The masculine form is used throughout these verses and in almost all cases the corresponding sexual partner is female. The laws therefore indirectly apply to the female equivalents. The odd one is verse 7: you (man) shall not uncover the nakedness of your father.

The 'prohibited degrees' are common to many cultures, though there are some variations. For example, some allow marriage to an uncle or aunt. The rationale for the law is disputed but the following reasons have been suggested.

It is not healthy to practise inbreeding (and the people knew this). There is a deep-seated feeling within human societies that it must be placed under a taboo. The only clue in the text itself is that verse 6 says 'no one may draw near to uncover the nakedness of his own flesh'.

The prohibitions in verses 17–18 are different in principle from the preceding ones. A man might marry a woman *or* her daughter, but not both. Possibly the thinking is that when a man marries a woman, they become 'one flesh' (compare v. 6) and so her kin ('flesh') become his kin, and therefore out of bounds. Note that Jacob's marriage to both Leah and Rachel would have been ruled out under this regulation. In the case of the two sisters, I wonder to what extent the word 'rival' gives the motivation for the law.

Whatever the rationale, the fact remains that these relationships were regarded as unclean and consequently forbidden. Notice that sexual intercourse is regulated by God. It is not permitted for two people to agree that they fancy each other and are not affecting anyone else if they want to have sex. There remains something very mysterious about this, that modern science has not fathomed, as far as I can tell.

REFLECTION

Disagreement continues on many issues and people often argue one side or the other for the wrong reasons and with a notable lack of respect for and appreciation of the other's convictions. We need to learn to disagree in love, even when we feel that huge dangers or huge injustices are involved.

27   LEVITICUS 19 (i)

GOOD BEHAVIOUR

Verse 18 is probably the best known of all Levitical verses: 'You shall love your neighbour as yourself.' Verse 34 is less well known but similar: 'You shall love the alien as yourself.' They deserve to be considered together because the context of the first is plainly 'Israelite kin and neighbours' and the second is 'outsiders'. The New Testament has lessened the distinction between the two groups, but not obliterated it. Even the most public-spirited people today recognize a primary responsibility to their family—at least their children (compare also Galatians 6:10). So verses 17–18 forbid hating a relative and *command* correction of a wrongdoing neighbour, with the warning that silence indicates condoning the wrong and becoming guilty. Taking vengeance and nursing a grudge are also strictly forbidden, and it is these things that are to be overcome by 'loving your neighbour as yourself'. Israelites are told that the alien must not be oppressed but treated as a citizen—as one of them—remembering that they had been aliens in Egypt. These two passages together indicate the two chief planks in biblical ethics:

- Remember what God is like ('I am Yahweh/the Lord...', vv. 12, 14, 16, 18, 28, 30, 32, 37).
- Remember what God has done (for you) ('...who brought you out of the land of Egypt', v. 36).

Both are suggested in the condensed phrase: 'I am the Lord your God' (vv. 3, 4, 10, 31). These ethical principles are emphasized time and time again throughout the book, and, in fact, in many other places in the Bible. The foundation is laid in Exodus 6:2–8, where the Lord announces that he will deliver the people from Egypt with signs and wonders and take them to himself to be his people: this reveals, more clearly than anything that has gone before, the meaning of the name 'Yahweh' (or 'the Lord').

The many other injunctions contained in this chapter spring from this basis. They may be grouped under a few headings.

- *Honesty in word, action and intention* (vv. 11–13, 15–16, 35–36). This rules out stealing, lying, cheating, swearing oaths falsely, exploitation, and dishonest business practices.

80

- *Concern for the vulnerable.* In verses 9–10 it is *commanded* that those with crops to harvest do not reap exhaustively. The poor are given the opportunity and the *right* to 'glean', that is, to gather what remains after the main reaping. Strict rules are given to employers with respect to the payment of wages. The deaf and blind are protected *by law* against abuse. They are not outside God's care and therefore a safe target, but under his special protection. The motive here, as in the famous verse 18, is love for the other person. It is a pity that the Church has been so slow to spot this forerunner of industrial and disability law. Doing good to the vulnerable is not an optional extra.

- *Respect for other people and God's creation.* Apart from the obvious commandments in verses 17–18 and 33–34, the motive of love for others is seen in verse 32. Many societies treat old people with respect, but there is always a temptation to despise or make fun of those who are getting older and weaker, and losing the abilities they once had.

- *Purity.* This covers single-mindedness with respect to God. Occult activity is outlawed (see the next reading) and flirting with foreign religious practices (vv. 26–28, 31; also 20:6, 27). It is probable that the commands against mixing animals, seeds and cloths are intended as a pointer to this principle (compare the kosher laws).

Sexual matters come under the heading of love for others too. It is unlikely that a man would deliberately make his daughter a prostitute unless there were the severest financial problems, but even then it is forbidden. Sex is a gift of God, not for resale but to be enjoyed within the guidelines that God himself has laid down.

This set of rules is quite comprehensive and covers both 'right-wing' and 'left-wing' concerns. We have probably all seen living caricatures—people who are strongly against sexual misconduct but think the poor have only themselves to blame, and scruffy marchers for social justice and free love. Leviticus suggests that both have an important point to make and both have limitations.

FOR REFLECTION

Do you unconsciously group these concerns in order of importance?
Are you giving all of them the weight that God expects?

WHICH LAWS APPLY *to* US?

It is so obvious that we are still required to 'love our neighbour as ourselves' that we may not consider why it is obvious. One rationale for deciding which Old Testament laws do still apply today has been to put laws into categories.

- The *moral laws*, which are binding for all time—killing, lying and stealing will always be wrong.

- The *ritual laws*, which are no longer applicable. For example, the sacrifices have been fulfilled and superseded by Christ's sacrifice on the cross, and the unclean food laws were declared void by Jesus in Mark 7:19 (compare Acts 10:15).

- The *social laws*, which were prescribed for Israel's time and place but which have to be modified for other situations. For example, the law prescribed the death penalty for adultery, whereas Jesus said, 'Let anyone among you who is without sin be the first to throw a stone' (John 8:7).

There is clearly some biblical support for this reasoning, but there are difficulties. First, the Old Testament never mentions any such division, and second, not all laws fit neatly into these categories. We have one such law under consideration here (sabbath keeping) and one in the following reading (homosexual relationships).

Evidence of slow progress

Verses 20–22 deal with the case of a man who has unlawful sexual relations with another man's slave woman. The penalty is a guilt offering of a ram. If she had been free, they would both have been put to death (as v. 20 implies and Deuteronomy 22:23–24 confirms). 'There is no longer slave or free' (Galatians 3:28) was a conviction yet undreamt of, and God seems to have been content to allow his people to learn bit-by-bit of his concern for all people. So, although the Israelites realized that 'even slaves had rights', there were refinements to the law still to come. The Old Testament law is not the last word on every subject.

The sabbaths: a difficult case

The motivation for the sabbath law seems to be partly humanitarian and partly religious: people need physical rest and time for worship. There have been two main views about Christians and the sabbath:

- It is necessary to keep Sunday, which has officially replaced the seventh day, as a day of rest. (Seventh Day Adventists, of course, believe that it is necessary to keep Saturday, the seventh day, free from work.) The law has never been scrapped.

- It is not necessary to keep any particular day as a day of rest, but the principle of achieving a rhythm of work and rest is a good one. The sabbath itself is never reiterated in the New Testament as necessary for Gentile Christians, not even in Acts 15:28–29.

There are many more involved arguments, and agreement has not been achieved. It is clear that we must make up our own minds and act accordingly, recognizing our own responsibility for reaching sincere conclusions. But there are problems in trying to work together for a common purpose. For example, what exactly should we be aiming for with respect to national law? Is there a way that Christians with differing viewpoints can work together effectively? The Keep Sunday Special campaign some years ago made progress in this in their attempts to persuade the government not to deregulate Sunday trading, even though they had limited success. Bearing in mind the fact that most people do not accept that the commandment to keep the sabbath came directly from God, there are still arguments that can be used. For example, people need to establish a rhythm of work and rest. It is good to have a particular day designated for rest and communal events (including worship). People should not be discriminated against for their religious convictions (although many employers are more likely to appoint those who are flexible in their availability for work).

FOR REFLECTION

Christians value Sunday as the day of resurrection and a day for God. Is there any future in trying to persuade the authorities to introduce further legislation to safeguard a weekly day of rest?

The OCCULT

Much of the material in this chapter is found elsewhere in Leviticus. The laws concerning incest (vv. 17–21) have the phrase 'sees… nakedness' (rather than 'uncovers', as in ch. 18) and include a reciprocal feature, 'and she sees his nakedness'. The meaning is the same, and the addition presumably emphasizes the fact that both parties are equally at fault. The penalty (as in 18:29) is to be 'cut off from their people'. This has been interpreted as meaning death by stoning, or banishment, or direct judgment of God in premature death or in not providing children to continue the line. This last judgment is spelt out in verses 20–21, but it is not clear whether it is meant to be the same as or different from the foregoing examples.

Offering children to Molech

Molech was the god of the Ammonites, though the actual name was 'Malch' or 'Malk'. The Hebrew writer has deliberately distorted it by giving it the wrong vowels, actually the vowels of *bosheth*, meaning 'shame', as in 'Ishbosheth' and 'Mephibosheth' (2 Samuel 2:8ff; 9:6ff). The phrase 'cause to pass (through/by/over) in the fire to Molech' occurs in Leviticus 18:21 (compare 2 Kings 23:10; Jeremiah 32:35) and refers either to sacrificing children on the altar or else to an ordeal by fire, signifying devotion or commitment to Molech. The former seems a more likely meaning of the words used, especially when Jeremiah talks about building the high place—a place for offering sacrifices—in order to do this abomination. Some have thought that Genesis 22, Abraham's 'nearly offering Isaac', indicates that child sacrifice was once practised in Israel. The Old Testament consistently denies this, but we may still see that in Abraham's world it would not have been as unthinkable as it is for us. Abraham proves his faith and devotion by his *willingness* to sacrifice his only son, but God provides a substitute. (See also the same concept in Numbers 3:40–41.) The people of the land are given the responsibility for seeing that these practices do not happen. Otherwise, God himself will 'set his face against them and their family and cut them off' (v. 5, the same penalty as for turning to wizards in v. 6).

'Helpful' occult practices ruled out

Verses 6 and 27 prohibit occult activity in the strongest terms (compare 19:26 and Deuteronomy 18:10–11, which has eight different expressions). The penalty for an occult practitioner is death by ston-ing. The practices mentioned in Deuteronomy 18 are not all clear. They include augury/divination (Joseph did it with a cup—unless he was kidding, Genesis 44:4–5), soothsaying (very uncertain meaning), consulting mediums (like the woman at Endor, who apparently brought up Samuel from the dead and would have been consulted on other matters), and wizards (who operate with familiar spirits—that is, they believe they have a 'spirit guide' who provides information not available to human senses). This area of experience is foreign to most in the West, but many Christians, especially in remote places, are closer to the experience of, for example, Samuel and Elisha (1 Samuel 9:5–10, 20; 2 Kings 4:27). People I have known who have dabbled in various occult activities, including apparently 'harmless fun', have had very bad experiences.

In many parts of Africa, spirit activity—to bring well-being or harm—is very much in evidence. Some Christians regard it as neutral and have become involved in it. Many Christians, on the other hand, testify to the wisdom of the biblical warnings against these practices. There are real dangers to physical and spiritual health. On the other hand, Christ is Lord over these powers and gives victory and deliverance.

FOR REFLECTION

If God prohibits something, may we assume that there are reasons for it—apart from an arbitrary test of obedience? If so, how will we set about finding those reasons?

MORE *about* SEX

We came across certain sexual regulations in chapter 18, which recur in chapter 20. We now concentrate on what was omitted in our comments there—intercourse during the woman's period (18:19; 20:18); sex between two men (women are not mentioned: 18:22; 20:13); and bestiality (18:23; 20:15–16). In the former chapter, no penalties are prescribed but chapter 20 decrees death for the latter two offences and being 'cut off from among their people' (v. 18) for the first. The difference in punishment suggests that anal intercourse and bestiality were regarded as more serious offences, but to be cut off, excluded from God's people, was a devastating penalty. It seems a hard judgment when probably most Christians today would not regard sex during a period as actually sinful. We noted that Leviticus 15:24, which prescribes only a time of purifying, may refer to sex without realizing that the period had started. A problem is raised, which seems to have no universally agreeable answer: what is the implication of the fact that these 'sexual regulations' both occur in the same section? Are they both abolished or both still in force? Or could one be OK and the other not?

Gay relationships

The problem of homosexual practice is felt to be particularly acute in many sections of the Church today. There are at least two major contrasting views here, and I believe they are both held with sincerity and sometimes anguish.

• The prohibition is meant for those times only, for it is found in a section following prohibitions against idolatry and occult practices. Together with the laws about bodily discharges, it is part of a symbolic system that serves as a powerful teaching aid about purity—wholehearted devotion to the Lord. (The same has been argued for Hindu laws of cleanliness: only a religious sanction would enable good practice to be enforced.) The sort of stable, loving homosexual relationships recommended by responsible gay people today were outside the experience of the ancient Israelites and not, therefore, intended to be addressed in Leviticus.

- The prohibition is valid permanently, since it is included among laws about incest and it is called an 'abomination'. Romans 1: 18–32 and 1 Corinthians 6:9–10 (and possibly 1 Timothy 1:8–11 and Jude 7) confirm that all homosexual practice—not just promiscuous behaviour—is off-limits for Christians.

Despite the disagreements, some things are incontrovertible. For instance, nothing is said about 'homosexual orientation', and celibate gays and lesbians should never have been discriminated against, as has unfortunately been the case in the Church. What kinds of sinners does God say we should not love? It is also true, whether or not the debate about 'genes or environment' can be resolved, that many, if not most, do not choose their sexual orientation.

Because of your hardness of heart?

Until comparatively recently, the mainline denominations refused to sanction remarriage after divorce. It is still the case that those in this position who wish to be ordained into the Anglican Church have to get special permission from the Archbishop and the circumstances of the divorce are investigated. There is, on the face of it, much clearer evidence in the New Testament against remarriage than against committed homosexual relationships. Could it be that they belong in the category of things that God allows because it is the best way for some people to manage their lives?

Those who are charged with forming policies and laws about gay and lesbian marriages, ordination of those in same-sex relationships, and so forth, face acutely difficult problems. Even those with no such responsibility need to sort out some difficult questions. What is the right view of homosexual practice? How should we relate to those who differ from us on this question? How do we try to prevent or discourage outlooks and practices that we feel to be harmful to vulnerable people and children?

FOR REFLECTION AND PRAYER

Many people who hold views contrary to our own put us to shame by the way they live. Give us, O Lord, the humility to seek your mind in truth and love, and the grace to speak and act accordingly.

PRIESTS, PURITY & PUNISHMENTS

The chapter deals with regulations for priests (vv. 1–9, 16–24) and for the high priest (vv. 10–15).

Priestly purity

To be a priest in Israel was a privilege and therefore involved stricter regulations and penalties for failure. Priests acted not only on their own behalf but as mediators between the people and God (vv. 6, 7b, 8), and as role models (v. 10). So they were not allowed to touch the dead bodies of anyone (the high priest was not even to go into the same room, v. 11) except mother or father (not even these for the high priest), son, daughter or virgin sister—possibly not even the body of his wife, although verse 4 is difficult to interpret. However, we should bear in mind the fact that the Old Testament laws allow for exceptions to be made under certain circumstances, as David recognized implicitly, Jesus clearly and the Pharisees reluctantly (1 Samuel 21:1–6; Matthew 12:2–5; cf. Numbers 28:9–10; Luke 13:10–17). It is important to grasp that the law was not given to be followed slavishly, but to guide the people in their attempts to please God. Verse 12 probably indicates that priestly duties took precedence over family ties (Wenham), certainly not that the priest had to spend all his life in the sanctuary.

Priests were also more restricted than normal in their choice of wife (v. 7), and the high priest even more so (vv. 13–15). The bride had to be a virgin—or, according to Ezekiel 44:22, the widow of a priest. It is not possible to know why this variation was introduced. Presumably, if two brothers were priests and one died, then the other would have the *duty* of taking his sister-in-law as wife in order to provide offspring for his brother (Deuteronomy 25:5–19). Again we note the implication that exceptions were allowed even when not stated explicitly.

Priests also had to fulfil physical criteria (vv. 17–21). One with a disability could eat of the holy and most holy things, and must, therefore, have been regarded as clean, but could not offer sacrifices as priest. This again is a ritual requirement which serves as a visual aid—but Jesus overruled it (see Matthew 21:12–14). We are no longer permitted to use physical disability as a symbol of spiritual uncleanness.

Prostitution and fornication

It is surprising that the law says very little about professional prostitution. It was not an acceptable profession in Israel and yet no punishment is laid down. We have several references to prostitutes which imply that they had a place in Israelite society and were regarded as more or less unavoidable.

Prostitution is often used as a metaphor for unfaithful religious behaviour. The word often translated 'prostitute' or 'harlot' is also used in a more general way of sexual intercourse outside marriage. Judah's daughter-in-law tricked him into having intercourse with her because he refused to give his last remaining son to help her produce a child. He wanted her put to death—the law of the time is not known, but the issue was that she was in effect committing adultery. Judah recognizes that she is more righteous than he (Genesis 38:14–26).

Deuteronomy 22:20–21 is the text that gives stoning as the penalty for adultery—mentioned by the men who tested Jesus in John 8:2–11. It has in view a woman who is found not to be a virgin by her new husband. It does not deal with the case of intercourse with a man who pays for sex with her, though it does condemn the act of 'prostituting herself in her father's house'. 1 Kings 3:16ff refers to two prostitutes who lived in the same house (a brothel?) who came to Solomon for a legal decision and received it. They were not stoned (there is probably no connection with the fact that Solomon had made eligible women scarce, 1 Kings 11:3).

The difference for a priest's daughter who 'defiles herself with respect to fornication or prostitution' (v. 9) is that she should 'be burned in or with the fire'. This probably means that she is burnt to death but it might just imply burning of her body after stoning. The New Testament contains several passages suggesting that the Old Testament law was not the last word on God's real requirements. Most would say that we have discovered at least some wrongs not specified in the New Testament, such as slavery. Are there likely to be more such discoveries in the years ahead?

FOR REFLECTION

Human beings look on the outward appearance but God looks on the heart (1 Samuel 16:7). Actually we do try to do better than judging only by outward appearance, so what is the difference between divine and human vision?

WHO EATS *the* PRIESTS' PORTIONS?

The first sentence of this chapter is puzzling: the priests are instructed to 'separate themselves from the holy things'. The 'holy things' are almost certainly the parts of sacrifices that belonged to the priests (see 7:30–36, referring to offerings of well-being or peace offerings). The word for 'separate' is from the same root as 'Nazirite', that is, a person dedicated to the Lord, separated off from ordinary people and forbidden to cut their hair or shave. Samson (Judges 13:4–5) apparently kept to this rule, although he was rather loose in his interpretation of other laws. The meaning here seems to be that priests are not automatically entitled to eat of the 'holy things': it is a privilege allowed under certain conditions only.

So the following are allowed to eat (vv. 1–9): priests and their families and slaves (who belong to the priest) who are in a clean state. They are excluded if they have a leprous disease or a discharge, or have touched an unclean swarming thing or dead body. In these latter cases, they are to wait until evening and wash before they are eligible to eat. And by the way, they are not to eat an animal that simply died or was killed by a wild animal (v. 8).

Explicitly excluded (vv. 10–13) are lay people (literally 'strangers, outsiders', that is, non-Levites), resident aliens, hired labourers and priest's daughters married to non-Levites.

The chiastic structure of these verses sets out the exclusions clearly.

a   v. 10: No lay person. No outsider.
   b   vv. 10b–11: No guest or hired labourer, although a bought slave may eat. No half-insider (neither fully lay nor fully priestly).
   b   vv. 12–13a: No priest's daughter married to a lay person, although a divorced or widowed daughter, returned to her father's house, may eat. No half-insider.
a   v. 13b: No lay person. No outsider.

Verses 17–20 imply that resident aliens could offer sacrifices. Verses 21–30 give further regulations about sacrifices of well-being (peace offerings), which may be either freewill offerings or vows (see comment on Leviticus 7:11–27, pp. 46–47). There is an unexpected difference here.

- Animals that are blind, injured, maimed, or having a discharge, itch, scab, or damaged testicles are not acceptable for either vows or freewill offerings.
- Animals with a limb too long or too short are OK for a freewill offering only.

Verse 25 rules out the possible excuse that an imperfect animal was bought from a foreigner and so it couldn't be helped.

Verses 26–30 deal with sacrificing young animals. There is a feeling in the Old Testament, revealed in several ways, that the bond between a mother and her offspring is sacred in some sense. See the command not to boil a kid in its mother's milk (Exodus 23:19; 34:26; Deuteronomy 14:21), which is possibly a protest against Canaanite practices, but possibly more than that. Perhaps it is something to do with the 'love' that exists between animals of different species, including goats as well as human beings.

On the face of it, this seems to be as irrelevant to our own situation as it could be. We have no hereditary priests, no sacrifices and therefore no sacrificial portions. Even the vicar's 'Easter Offering' (traditionally, the Easter collections in the Church of England went to the vicar) is regulated by the taxman and not the Old Testament. Yet the section does confirm the important truth that a married woman no longer belongs with parents but with her husband. The situation is similar for a married man, as is explicitly stated in Genesis 2:24. The parents have therefore no *right* to interfere, and the married son or daughter has no *right* to expect food or shelter with parents— although both parties retain the right to give freely and joyfully.

We now believe that we can enter into God's presence boldly through the sacrifice of Christ (Hebrews 4:14–16), yet Leviticus 22 warns us of the seriousness of what we do and reminds us that this privilege is not an essential right but a hard-won gift. The difference between sinful human beings and the holy God remains as awesome as ever.

A CHALLENGE

'You shall not offer anything that has a blemish' (v. 20).

33 LEVITICUS 23

A Liturgical Calendar

This chapter provides a handy diary or crib sheet for priests and other Israelites, a brief summary of the dates and requirements of the principal feasts. The contents go like this.

The checklist

These are the appointed festivals. Make them known and keep them. Incidentally, don't forget that the sabbath goes on all the time (vv. 1–3).

- **Passover, 14.1** (fourteenth day of the first month—that is, Abib or Nisan, March–April) at twilight (v. 5).

- **Unleavened Bread, 15.1**, lasting for seven days (vv. 6–8).

- **First fruits** (first day of the week, after the first crops are harvested and before any are used). The sheaf is brought to the priest, who raises it before the Lord; also on the same day, a burnt offering of a one-year-old lamb plus cereal and drink offerings (vv. 9–14).

- **Feast of Weeks or Pentecost** (seven weeks later, on the first day of the week again). Lasts fifty days counting both the first and last Sundays. Two leavened loaves plus seven yearling lambs, one bullock and two rams (plus cereal and drink offerings), all as a burnt offering; plus one male goat and two male yearling lambs as a wave offering (a type of peace offering) (vv. 15–21).

- **Gleaning law**. Leave part of your crop for the poor to gather (v. 22).

- **Trumpets, 1.7** (Ethanim or Tishri, that is, September–October). Do no work but do present your sacrifices (vv. 23–25).

- **Evening of 9.7**. Do no work, in preparation for the following day (v. 32).

- **Day of Atonement, 10.7** (*Yom Kippur*: see comment on Leviticus 16, pp. 72–75). There is strong emphasis on not working, the penalty being to 'be cut off' or 'be destroyed' (vv. 26–32).

- **Feast of Booths, 15–22.7** (*Sukkoth* = *Tabernacles*) for seven days plus a sabbath on the eighth day (vv. 33–36). The people live in booths for seven days to remember how they lived when they came out of Egypt (vv. 39–43).

Closing summary: the aforementioned are the appointed festivals. There are also sabbaths, votive offerings and freewill offerings (vv. 37–38). Thus Moses declared the appointed festivals to the people (v. 44).

A holy convocation

Holy convocation/convention ('a calling of holiness') is mentioned eleven times in this chapter. It signifies a festival that was announced publicly. In later Judaism it was the Sanhedrin's responsibility to proclaim these festivals. 'Holy' signifies that it was 'set apart' for the service of God. It is perhaps surprising that, in most references to the sabbath, there is no mention of worship. Verse 3, however, confirms that we are right to assume the connection between rest and worship (convocation).

'You (*plural*) shall bring *from your settlements*,' says verse 17. The word translated 'settlements' (moshab) is used rather generally and it is not clear what size of unit is meant here. This festival comes after the harvest and would be more lavish than usual, but it is unlikely that each family would really be expected to give seven lambs, a bullock and two rams to be completely consumed as a burnt offering. Perhaps, therefore, it signifies the offering of an extended family or larger group within each tribe.

Scholars have observed how two loaves (a rather modest requirement) are mentioned first (v. 17), and then the animals are almost tacked on. 'Offer with the bread...' sounds a bit like, 'The subscription will cost 75 pence... and £700'. We recall that certain provisions were made for those who were too poor to offer the normal prescribed offerings (two turtle doves instead of a lamb), so we presume that those who did not have the wherewithal would not be expected to offer these sacrifices at the Feast of Weeks.

FOR REFLECTION

*What, if anything, does the study of this Old Testament background
add to our insight into the meaning of Christian faith and living?
Is it helpful to continue to keep certain times of the year
for particular emphases?*

The NIGHT LIGHT & *the* LOAVES

The lamp kept burning in the holy place and the 'shewbread' are both referred to in 1 Samuel (3:3; 21:4–6) and belong to the earliest period of Israel's history.

The lamp

Flames and fire have many connotations in religion. Parsees always keep a 'sacred flame' burning in a massive urn within their temple. Hindus celebrate the festival of light—*Diwali* or *Deepavali* (or other variants). A fire may signify burning judgment, as when God wiped out the cities of Sodom and Gomorrah with 'fire and brimstone (sulphur)' (Genesis 19:24). It may signify purification through testing as in Isaiah 1:25–26 and Zechariah 13:9, or simply purification as in Isaiah 6:6–7, when Isaiah's lips were cleansed by a burning coal from the altar. Fire may represent the awesome majesty of God, as when Moses ascended Mount Sinai to receive the ten commandments (Exodus 19:18, compare the thunder and lightning in Exodus 19:16 and possibly the burning bush in 3:2–4). The flame of a lamp gives light rather than heat and signifies both understanding the truth ('lead us from darkness to light') and obedience ('walk in the light').

The Israelites had something smaller than the Parsees, but there was still an obligation to keep it burning, at least through the night hours (vv. 2–4; cf. Exodus 27:20–21; 30:7). The lampstand had to be of pure gold and the oil used as fuel had to be pure. This suggests that the significance was something like 'the pure light of God' in the place where his presence was celebrated. The lamp was apparently not lit during daylight hours (see v. 3, 'from evening to morning'), when the ordinary symbols of the tabernacle or temple could be seen: compare the differing signs that God provided for the Israelites in their desert wanderings, a pillar of cloud by day and a pillar of fire by night (Exodus 13:21–22).

The lamp is mentioned almost incidentally in 1 Samuel 3:3: 'the lamp of God had not yet gone out'. This probably means that it was early morning and still dark.

The shewbread

The shewbread is described in verses 5–9. These twelve loaves were placed before the Lord every sabbath, and presumably the previous week's bread was removed and eaten by the priests (Aaron's descendants) 'in a holy place' (v. 9). This probably signifies either a place within the area of the tent of meeting or (later) the temple, or else somewhere not 'outside the camp' (where unclean or unwanted things were disposed of or banished, as we have seen in 4:12, 21; 8:17).

We know from the incident in Mark 2:23–28 that Jesus regarded this law as relative and capable of being superseded by a more important consideration. So, when he is accused of violating the sabbath, he refers to the time when David and his men, when they were very hungry, ate the shewbread that was reserved for the priests (1 Samuel 21:4–6). This is an important passage because it shows us how other Old Testament laws might be regarded—not as absolute rules to be carried out irrespective of the human factors involved, but as indications of what God requires under normal circumstances. Of course, there is a danger in saying this, that we go to the opposite extreme and take a very light view of the commandments laid down in the Old Testament. We should remind ourselves, therefore, of places such as the Sermon on the Mount where Jesus makes these laws even more demanding: not only is murder wrong, but the attitudes that lead to it (for example, anger and scorn for a fellow human being); similarly with stealing, adultery and so on.

The lamp was placed in the holy place together with the altar of incense and the table with the shewbread, just outside the holy of holies. So it was available to the priests alone and its symbolism was intended to instruct them. Sometimes people today feel that the 'sanctuary' of a church building is more holy than elsewhere, or that the 'reserved sacrament' (bread blessed by the priest for holy communion) sanctifies a particular place. Is this in line with the thinking of both Old and New Testaments or is it something that has now been superseded? (Consider Matthew 27:51; Hebrews 4:14–15; 1 Peter 2:5, 9.)

FOR REFLECTION

Reflect on the meaning of light and heat. Then light a candle—or, better still, light or find a fire—and reflect again. What advantage is there in actually having something to see and feel when meditating?

35 LEVITICUS 24:10–23

DEATH *to* ALL BLASPHEMERS

The present section has a very contemporary feel to it, for many Muslim countries have strict blasphemy laws, often carrying the death penalty. In Britain no one could have been unaware of the case of Salman Rushdie and the *fatwa* ('ruling on a point of Islamic law by a recognized authority') concerning him, namely that he should be killed because of what he had written in *The Satanic Verses*. There are reports, too, of the law's being misused by those who bring false accusations in order to harm someone, as was the case with Naboth (1 Kings 21:10; see below) and, of course, Jesus and the first Christian martyr, Stephen (Matthew 26:65–66; Acts 6:11ff).

Let's first note some features of the text. The presenting problem is the case of a man who is Israelite on his mother's side and Egyptian on his father's, who 'blasphemes the Name in a curse'. We cannot be sure of the meaning of the word translated 'blaspheme' in this chapter (*naqab*), but it certainly implies something negative and destructive. It has the same form as a word meaning 'pierce' and might be formed from a word meaning 'curse'. This, together with the context ('in a curse'), shows that we are on the right track: perhaps the blasphemer is asserting that 'the Lord is not as his name implies' (George Knight). This would undermine the people's faith— suggesting that what they believed about God was wrong.

There is no commandment that says, 'You shall not blaspheme the Name...' but the second commandment says, 'You shall not take the Name of the Lord your God in vain'—literally 'not lift up... to vanity, emptiness'. A more common word for 'blaspheme' (*gadaph*) means 'revile' and is used of person-to-person abuse in Psalm 44:16. The charge against Naboth was that he had 'reviled' or 'cursed' God and the king (1 Kings 21:9–10). 2 Kings 19:22 gives further insight into how blasphemy was understood, where the Assyrians allege that the Lord is the same as all the other gods and unable to save Judah from defeat. Ezekiel 20:27 describes a case of blasphemy by 'dealing treacherously' with God and worshipping idols.

So it seems that 'blasphemy' covered a wide range of offences, all connected with saying, by word or deed, things about God which are not true. The new issue, here in chapter 24, is whether this offence applies to those who are not native Israelites. The procedure followed illustrates how case law was built up in Old Testament times. They laid the problem before God and waited for guidance (v. 12). In this case we are given a specific decision (death by stoning) plus two general principles to help with cases that are related but different:

- Anyone who curses God shall bear the sin... be put to death (vv. 15–16).
- There is one law for alien and Israelite (citizen) alike (v. 22).

Could even Moses hear God's voice sufficiently clearly to discern his perfect will? For Christians, there is a strict warning about applying the same penalties nowadays. The law of Moses commanded that adulterers should be put to death, but Jesus overruled this in John 8:7, 'Let the one who is without sin cast the first stone.'

It is interesting that the form of verses 14–23 is chiastic, with a very clear (and apparently unnecessary) repetition of verses 17 and 18 (the same as 21b and 21a). This indicates a strong emphasis on the middle principle: eye for eye and tooth for tooth. It is like this:

a Blasphemy is punishable by death—one law for citizen and alien.
  b Killing a human being is punishable by death.
    c Killing an animal requires restitution.
      d Principle of like for like (*lex talionis*).
    c Killing an animal requires restitution.
  b Killing a human being is punishable by death.
a One law for citizen and alien—the blasphemer is put to death.

What, then, is our response to blasphemy today? How should we evaluate the Muslim position, which seems to have so much in common with Old Testament law? Personally, I find it very painful to hear the name Christ used as an expletive—much more painful than four-letter-word swearing. Is it possible to communicate that pain without exhibiting a judgmental or self-righteous attitude, but bearing witness to God's gracious love and forbearance?

FOR REFLECTION

What should our attitude be towards blasphemy of various types today? Should there be regulation by law? Have you anything to pass on to your MP? Have you written letters, both appreciative and critical, to the media?

36   LEVITICUS 25:1–24

The YEAR *of* JUBILEE

It is this section of Leviticus that inspired Jubilee 2000, the campaign to persuade governments and banks to release the poorest countries of the world from their crippling debts. It was a massive effort by a number of Christian and other agencies to motivate people to write to MPs and other officials, to demonstrate and to attend meetings, to study the issues so as to be able to speak accurately, knowledgeably and persuasively. The campaign did indeed have strong justification from Leviticus 25.

The system laid out was this:

Years 1–7:   Six years of normal sowing, then one sabbath year.
Years 8–49: The same pattern repeated six more times.
Year 50:   A sabbatical year (following on directly from sabbatical year 49).

In a normal sabbatical year, in which crops were not sown and vineyards were not pruned, the previous harvest had to last two years instead of one. This must have been very difficult at times, so we can imagine the dismay felt by some at the prospect of two consecutive sabbaticals. How would they make one harvest last for three years? There are two answers.

- God allows people (and animals) to eat what grows up without having been deliberately planted (vv. 6–7).

- God promises a bumper harvest in year 48 to last for three years (v. 21).

People have always found it difficult to trust God in such practical matters. That is presumably why we are amazed at the practical faith of people like George Muller, Hudson Taylor and, in our own time, Jackie Pullinger-To. What is not obvious when reading inspiring stories is the hardship that often goes with trusting God. But it is surprising that there is no reference to the jubilee or even the sabbatical year in any of the *narrative* passages of the Old Testament. This has caused scholars to ask whether it was ever kept, even whether it was simply a late addition to the law, expressing a pious hope and un-

98

realizable ideal. Your opinion of that view will depend on your overall view of scripture, since arguments from silence are notoriously unreliable. It is surprising, for example, that we have no references to the schooling system in Israel, apart from the exhortations to teach your children by instruction, discipline and the use of visual aids, sometimes intended to prompt questions (see Joshua 4:6–7, 21–24; also Deuteronomy 27:5–8; Joshua 10:27; 24:26–27).

Particular temptations would be to try to provide extra insurance (as today), to refuse to take on a bad risk, to exploit the weakness of the bargaining position of the poor. These practices are to some extent anticipated and legislated against. However, the law can never produce the whole-hearted and joyful obedience that God expects of us. There are exhortations in the Old Testament to this kind of response, and from time to time prophets expounded God's intentions and pointed out how particular practices were contrary to the law. Amos, for example, lashes people who combine outward piety with unjust practices, who 'lay themselves down by every altar on garments taken in pledge...' (Amos 2:8; compare Deuteronomy 24:12–13). Hosea and Micah outline God's attitude in a positive way: 'I desire steadfast love and not sacrifice, the knowledge of God rather than burnt offerings' and 'What does the Lord require of you but to do justice, and to love kindness, and to walk humbly with your God?' (Hosea 6:6; Micah 6:8).

It is clear today that for many people, criticism is out and fun is in. They will respond well to fund-raising events like Comic Relief, aimed at doing something positive for those in need. Often they will give sacrificially of their time to things that they become concerned about. But they don't like to be told what they ought to do. On the other hand, the religious groups growing fastest are often those that do tell people what to believe and how to behave. These extremes exhibit both strength and weakness. Is there some way of demonstrating that it is a joyful thing to serve God wholeheartedly, without minimizing the note of sacrifice and counting the cost that Jesus spoke about?

FOR REFLECTION

The jubilee year was a sacrament of liberty, proclaiming at the
same time social justice, authentic worship, personal holiness,
and confirmation of God's commitment to his people
(25:55; compare Isaiah 61:1–2).

The PRINCIPLE *of* REDEMPTION

Land in Israel was supposed to remain in the family. It was regarded as having been allotted to the various tribes of Israel at the time of the conquest under Joshua, although the process of large numbers of people taking over an area of land is bound to be very compli-cated and any account of it must be simplified. We know that there were many anomalies and irregularities in the early days of the nation (see Judges 1; 17—18) but, somehow or other, land was dis-tributed and each parcel was regarded as belonging to a particular extended family. The incident with Naboth illustrates this well: 'The Lord forbid that I should give you my ancestral inheritance' (1 Kings 21:3). So the law forbade the permanent transfer of land from one family to another. Land actually belonged to God who leased it to the Israelites and reserved the right to say what happened to it. At the jubilee, land was to return to its 'original' occupants. Con-sequently the price of land fluctuated according to how near the jubilee was, in much the same way as the value of leasehold prop-erty fluctuates today.

When land was sold, it could be redeemed at any time, either by the person who had sold it or by a 'next of kin'. We do not know the exact rules or traditions governing the right of redemption but we have the story of Boaz, who redeemed Naomi's land, sold many years beforehand when the family moved to Moab, and was therefore expected (apparently) to marry Ruth (Ruth 3:1–2, 9–13; 4:1–12). Clearly this provision would also affect the willingness of anyone to buy land and make improvements on it, and no doubt some hard bargaining took place.

Houses in cities

Houses in walled cities (vv. 29–34) could only be redeemed up to a year after their sale. After that, the buyer had the freehold. Houses in open villages and houses belonging to Levites, even in cities, could be redeemed at any time, and reverted to the original owner in the jubilee year. So there is a particular and limited change of status for the area of a city within walls. This is also seen in Numbers 35, which sets out the regulations regarding Levitical cities, including the cities of refuge. Land around walled cities is not to be swallowed up by urban expansion: it remains redeemable at all times.

Those in difficulties

Israelites were required (by law, note) to treat other Israelites as their brothers and sisters, as fellow human beings brought out of Egypt by God, redeemed from bondage, saved from oppression (vv. 35–46). The kind of lending condemned rules out the exploitation of dire need but not necessarily lending for business purposes.

Verses 47–55 deal with the case of a resident alien who becomes wealthy and able to hire Israelites. The regulations allow these foreigners to prosper. In the jubilee year, they would presumably not be able to hold on to either bonded labour or land, but there would always be people who needed help and had land to sell. When you got your land back, you might have to remortgage it in order to pay debts of setting-up expenses.

The dependants of Israelites (vv. 35, 39) were those who were unable to support themselves and asked for food and shelter from their relatives. God commands that these people should not be treated as slaves (who 'belonged to' their owner), but he allows foreigners to be slaves. In this we can see, as in many other Old Testament laws, both a significant and difficult step forward and an inadequacy. It is to the shame of the Christian Church that, for centuries, it could even allow the enslavement of fellow Christians without realizing the repugnant nature of this practice.

Differing responsibilities today

The issue of how 'foreigners' are treated is not all that simple. We can easily criticize the division between Israelites and resident aliens in that it seems to put the latter into a lower category of humanity: they may, for instance, be enslaved. But the New Testament recognizes that we have different duties to different people. 'Let us work for the good of all, and especially for those of the family of faith' (Galatians 6:10).

QUESTION

How do our responsibilities differ towards different people and groups—our children (when young and old), parents, fellow Christians, fellow countrymen and so on?

38 LEVITICUS 26:1-13

OBEDIENCE & BLESSING

We are nearing the end of the book of Leviticus, and this chapter gives us a summary of the results of obedience and disobedience. These 'results' have been given different nuances by different readers, scholars and groups. Are they inducements to good behaviour and threats for the rebellious? Are they gracious promises and salutary warnings? Do they give a basis for the 'prosperity gospel'—the idea that Christians who are faithful to God may obtain material blessings as well as spiritual, and be free from physical harm?

Physical and spiritual benefits

Starting with what we can be sure of, material blessing is *in some way* linked with obedience. The New Testament confirms this in various ways: 'Seek first his kingdom and his righteousness, and all these things [food and clothing] will be given to you as well' (Matthew 6:33, NIV), and 'If in my name you ask me for anything, I will do it' (John 14:14).

We might also note Mark 10:28–30, but look at the ending! 'There is no one who has left house or brothers or sisters... who will not receive a hundredfold now in this age—houses, brothers and sisters... *with persecutions*. And we note also John 16:33: 'In the world you face persecution.'

So there are reasons to question a straight equation of obedience and material blessing. In the Old Testament, the book of Job is the clearest indication of the fact that those who are righteous may suffer terribly. But this is not all. Many of the prophets suffered simply *because* they were righteous, and Jesus was the climax of this pattern.

We do not find much about 'spiritual blessing' in the Old Testament. Material blessings are *generally* taken to be signs of God's attitude towards those who experience them, so we must make two important points:

- Physical well-being is not just physical but a sign of something more important.

- There is no exact correlation between righteousness and material blessings.

Blessings and danger

The case of Solomon is very odd. In answer to an open invitation, he asked for wisdom (1 Kings 3:9). God was pleased with his request, granted it, and gave wealth as an added bonus. But Solomon ended up a very foolish man (1 Kings 11:9–11). I wonder to what extent the wealth contributed to his mistakes. The gifts that God himself gives, including talents, can become a snare. A gift from God carries with it a responsibility to use it rightly, and many gifts are dangerous.

Having looked at some of the issues raised by this chapter, we can see that it has much in common with the teaching of Jesus. It starts with a warning against idolatry and emphasizes the fact that the Lord (Yahweh) is the one who addresses them and who is their God. Note the repeated 'I am Yahweh' in verses 2–3; also verse 12 and, at the very end of the chapter, verses 44–45. This theme therefore makes a strong framework for the whole chapter and indicates a most important overriding and constant consideration. From this clear focus on the one God will flow blessing and protection ('Seek first the kingdom... and all these things will be added').

Verse 12 is an important theological statement. It alludes to the great promise made to Moses in Exodus 6:2–8, when God promised to reveal the significance of the name Yahweh: he would bring the people out of Egypt, redeem them from the house of bondage with mighty acts of judgment, and would *take them to be his people*. God's presence in the midst of his people is the most important blessing and the strongest guarantee of the people's final security (compare also Ezekiel 43:7, 9; Zechariah 2:10–11; 8:3–8).

Overall, this chapter recognizes that human beings do not receive a wonderful gift and live happily (and obediently) ever after. Deuteronomy is even more emphatic in linking wealth to pride and subsequent disobedience. When the Israelites do disobey, God will discipline them severely (26:14–39). Nevertheless, the way back to God via repentance is always open (26:40–45). He is, after all, their God who redeemed them.

FOR REFLECTION

What justification could there for praying for wealth? How could anyone be sure about their motives?

39 LEVITICUS 26:14–46

SEVERE PUNISHMENT *but a* WAY BACK

A casual look through this chapter might give the impression of a vindictive God with a whole list of unpleasant things ready for recalcitrant sinners. The pattern is, 'If you don't respond to A, I'll send B, and if you don't respond to B...' So the list consists of:

A Terror and sickness (v. 16a); poor harvests (v. 16b, cf. 19, 20); defeat and occupation by enemies (v. 17).

B Sevenfold punishment (v. 18); hard sky and earth (v. 19, see below); hard labour for no result (v. 20).

C Sevenfold punishment (v. 21); death and loss of livestock through wild animals (v. 22, cf. Deuteronomy 7:22).

D Sevenfold punishment (v. 24); invasion, siege and disease (vv. 23–25; famine (v. 26).

E Sevenfold punishment (v. 28); the severest possible famine (v. 29); destruction of places of unauthorized worship and many dead and unable to be buried (v. 30); complete devastation of the land, causing sacrifice to cease (vv. 31–32); and exile (v. 33).

F Even those who survive all this will continue to have problems— 'utter demoralization' (D. Kidner) (vv. 36–39).

The number seven in the Bible often signifies completeness in some way, especially in the completion of creation portrayed in seven days, and also the many occurrences of 'sevenfold judgment' in the book of Revelation (for example, seven bowls and trumpets). The 'sky as iron and the land as brass' (v. 19) probably signifies lack of rain, producing a hard and unproductive earth.

It is clear, however, that God's motive for these judgments is to bring the people to their senses so that they will repent and turn back to the Lord. There will be no need for stage two if the people repent after stage one. There is a similar pattern of judgments in Amos 4:6–11, with the repeating refrain, 'Yet you did not return to me, says the Lord.'

The final section gives the Lord's real desire—that the people should confess their wrongdoing and turn from it. Despite their unfaithfulness, God will remain faithful to his covenant and will restore. He will not 'spurn... abhor... destroy them utterly' (v. 44). But why should they confess the iniquity of their ancestors? (v. 40).

What is the point of the metaphor of the land 'enjoying its sabbaths' (v. 34)? A more literal translation would be 'pay off (or be paid for) its sabbaths'. It is clear that land benefits from a sabbath, or fallow year, and becomes worn out and unproductive if it is expected to go on year after year. In one sense, this is simply a vivid metaphor or personification. However, the fact that the land did not have its sabbaths (v. 35) implies that the people did not keep the law, and that means that they had no regard for the poor of the land. If the year of jubilee was also neglected, then this amounts to blatant stealing from the people to whom the land should have been returned, and so stealing from God himself.

There are two contrasting surprises in these verses. First, it is unfashionable to speak in such harsh terms about God's direct punishment of a people. Sufferings are described here which many would 'not wish upon their worst enemy'. We may reasonably object that it would be more satisfactory to say that God *allows* such things, but the problem is not removed completely, for God, the ruler of the world, *could have* overruled.

Second, despite the deliberate and determined sinfulness of the people that is described in verses 14–39, which might well justify Sodom-and-Gomorrah treatment, God still promises to accept them back. They are still the people with whom he has made a covenant, and he will never forget that.

These two items together add up to stupendous news. God relentlessly pursues those who set themselves against him in arrogant pride, never pretending that their behaviour is 'understandable in one sense' or 'not so bad really'. Yet at the end he accepts the worst and overcomes it with his grace. These same features are part of the gospel displayed in the New Testament. Jesus himself asked, 'Do you think that… they were worse sinners than all other Galileans? No, I tell you; but unless you repent, you will all perish as they did' (Luke 13:2–3). Sin against God is never downplayed in the New Testament but regarded as, if possible, even more horrible than in the Old. Certainly it is more universal and inescapable (see Romans 3:21–26). But do you detect a shift of emphasis in Romans?

FOR MEDITATION

'In his anguish he prayed more earnestly, and his sweat became like great drops of blood falling down on the ground.'

Luke 22:44

VOWING & CHANGING YOUR MIND

Verses 1–8 specify the money that must be paid to release an individual from an explicit vow. Animals, property and land could also be both dedicated to the Lord and bought back by paying their value plus twenty per cent.

Various release fees

Probably the first thing to strike readers of these verses today, at least in the West, is the different values attached to different classes of people. A ready-reckoner for priests might look like this:

Age range	Price in shekels	
	Male	Female
1 month to 5 years:	5	3
5 to 20 years:	20	10
20 to 60 years:	50	30
over 60 years:	15	10
too poor for the above:	priest's assessment	

This seems to envisage a situation where, for example, a man might dedicate himself or one of his dependants to the Lord. The boy Samuel was dedicated in this way in 1 Samuel 1:21–28 and became a servant of God in the place of worship and sacrifice at Shiloh, under the tutelage of Eli the priest. The law in Leviticus 27 would make it possible for Hannah and Elkanah, his parents, to have taken the boy back but paid to the priest either 5 or 20 shekels (depending on his age at the time, 1 Samuel 1:22). If a man had vowed that he himself would, in effect, become a slave of God, he would pay 50 shekels, about the same as 50 months' wages for a labourer. See also comment on Numbers 6:1–21 (pp. 118–119) and Numbers 30 (pp. 174–175).

Equal—but how equal?

Since the concept of the fees is related to wages for work as a bonded labourer, it is to be expected that the price will vary according to the perceived productivity of the person bought or sold. The table above looks like a rather blunt instrument! Perhaps this goes some way towards making the point that people are equal and not just commodities, but it is clear that the Old Testament does not go the whole hog in demonstrating equality. Why should that be, in view of the fact that God knew about the sentiments of Galatians 3:28 long before the time of Moses? We shall see again and again that laws are presented in the Pentateuch that we could easily 'improve upon'.

The ban: no release

In verses 28–29 we find another reference to 'devoting to destruction' ('putting to the ban'). If persons (that is, enemies to be conquered) have been put under this judgment, there is to be no escape from it, but there is actually some latitude with regard to the spoil (animals and things). This might be devoted to destruction (as in Joshua 6:17, 21; 1 Samuel 15:3) or not (as in Deuteronomy 2:34–35; 3:6–7), according to the seriousness of the situation. Once placed under the ban, however, it could not be rescued.

As we have seen previously, there are different ways of responding to laws which we now find difficult.

- The Old Testament represents what people *thought* God required, but their understanding was imperfect and we need to reject or correct inadequate regulations.

- God went along gently with people, starting where they were and with what they could (more or less) accept. He did not force them to learn too much too quickly but educated them over many centuries.

Either way, we now recognize that the Old Testament is not the last word on many subjects and we must look to the New Testament for further clarification. We have also been given minds to discover further facts about God's world and therefore the effects of various actions.

FOR REFLECTION

'Everyone in this firm is as important as anyone else... But it's easier to replace the cleaner than the chief sales rep.' In what ways are people equal or unequal? In what ways might the cleaner be more important (not just less of a pain) than the chief sales rep?

An AUTHORIZED CENSUS

When is a census commanded or forbidden by God? The answer seems to be, 'It's OK when it's *his* idea'. Readers who have already come across David's disastrous census in 2 Samuel 24 (also in 1 Chronicles 21) will be surprised to find that the Lord actually commands Moses to number the people of Israel here. (See also the comment on Numbers 3, pp. 112–113.) The motive here is to find how many men there are who are at least twenty years old and able to fight. During this period of the nation's history, battle capacity was at the forefront of their minds. One might think that taking a census just before a series of military encounters is a bad time to choose! Perhaps the implication is that even those who were to lose their lives in battle were actually a part of the people of Israel.

Millions on the march?

The numbers given in this chapter have understandably given problems to all but the most miracle-minded of commentators and general readers. A company of over 600,000 men probably indicates over two million people when we take into account wives and children too. If you think of an area that you know containing this number of people and try to imagine them all on a march in the desert (or anywhere), it's extremely difficult. It's true that several million fled from East Pakistan (now Bangladesh) in 1971, but it took a massive international effort to try to meet their needs. They were not co-ordinated and no one could have addressed them as one body. Therefore, many scholars have asked whether these numbers are to be taken at face value, or whether they are symbolic in some way, or whether mistakes have occurred in transmission—or whether they were plucked out of someone's imagination in the first place. There are some noteworthy features and some facts that might indicate a possible solution.

There is a word with the same consonants as the Hebrew word for 'thousand' that means a 'chief', possibly the leader of a smallish group of some sort—conjectures range from a family group or a tent group to a military unit. It is possible that there was some confusion in the minds of later scribes who took 'leader of a smallish group' to mean 'one thousand'.

If we consider the numbers of thousands separately from the numbers of the hundreds and tens, we notice that the thousands range between 32 and 74, and the hundreds and tens range between 200 and 700, but seven of the twelve tribes have either 400 or 500. Statistically we should expect the hundreds to be more evenly distributed, and this could suggest that the hundreds and tens are not simply random but give the total numbers in each tribe. To take Reuben as an example (46,500), we could say that the tribe consisted of a total of 500 men, divided into 46 smallish groups. The average number in each of these groups would be 10.8. The same calculation applied to each tribe shows average group sizes of between 5.1 and 14.4.

So, we could interpret the text as meaning that there were 598 smallish groups (each with a chief) and a total population of 5550 Israelite men who were fit to fight. If a later scribe added together 598,000 and 5550, he would have made the number given in verse 46 —603,550.

Getting the numbers right

The reasoning here is not simply of academic interest because it affects our view of how the text of the Bible came into existence and was transmitted. Those with a very conservative view of scripture usually speak of the complete reliability of the biblical text *as originally given*, and accept that mistakes in copying have occurred along the way. Indeed, there is no disputing this, because there are many thousands of differences (usually small and insignificant) in the manuscripts we possess. There is no surviving original manuscript of either the Old Testament or the New.

More importantly, it also affects the way we *imagine* the people of Israel in the desert and Moses, and probably all who enjoy a good story need a plausible image for the imagination.

We shall come across other numerical details and will pick up the story later. For now, ask yourself what difference it makes to you whether the biblical text can be regarded as historical and capable of being explained plausibly to those who find the Old Testament frankly unbelievable (in a negative sense).

MEDITATION

One in a thousand or one in a million: each is individually known by God and very precious.

LEVITES & *the* TABERNACLE

Camping arrangements

The bulk of this section, in terms of text, describes the arrangement of the tribes when they camped. It is most easily grasped—and quicker to study, skim or even completely ignore—by means of a diagram. The numbers given are the 'thousands' or 'chiefs of groups' and then the number arrived at by adding up the figures for the hundreds and tens.

North
Dan, Asher, Naphtali (vv. 25–31)
(62+41+53K=156K; 1600 total?)

	Ephraim, Manasseh, Benjamin	Tent of Meeting	Judah, Issachar, Zebulun	
West	(vv. 18–24) (40+32+35K =107K; 1100 total?)	and Levites (vv. 3–9)	(v. 17) (74+57+54K =185K; 1400 total?)	**East**

Reuben, Simeon, Gad (vv. 10–16)
(46+59+45K=150K; 1450 total?)
South

The grouping of the tribes is the same in chapter 2 as in chapter 1, but the order is different. The obvious symbolism here is that the ark represents God's presence 'in the midst' (or centre) of the camp. This phrase is used at significant times in the Old Testament. For example, in Zechariah 8:3, describing the restoration of the people of Judah after a time of punishment in exile, the Lord says, 'I will return to Zion, and will dwell in the midst of Jerusalem…'

The names of leaders are given, which strengthens the case for arguing that these are genuine records of actual events in history, but they are unlikely to be of much interest except to highly specialized researchers.

Danger: God

The Levites are singled out for comment. They are not to be enrolled in the census (1:49; 2:33—but they were counted—see chapter 3). Their task is different from that of the battle-ready males enrolled (1:1–46). They are to take charge of the tabernacle and everything pertaining to it. They are also commanded to encamp around the tabernacle of the covenant in order that *there may be no wrath on the congregation* (1:53).

The idea that it is dangerous to get too close to God appears several times in the Old Testament. The most illuminating is probably Moses' conversation with the Lord when he asks, 'Show me your ways, so that I may know you and find favour in your sight' and 'Show me your glory' (Exodus 33:13, 18). God promises to 'proclaim his name, Yahweh', before Moses (which he does, giving the significance of it, Exodus 34:6–7) and to let Moses see his back after he has passed by, because 'no one shall see me and live' (33:20). The story of how Moses' face shone, after he had been speaking with God, makes the same sort of point. God's glory is overwhelming and the Israelites could not even look at Moses' face after he had spoken to God. Incidentally, notice that writers use different types of language in speaking of God: Isaiah says 'I saw the Lord', but this does not necessarily contradict what is said in Exodus. Ezekiel could never have brought himself to copy Isaiah's blunt language: he saw '*the appearance of the likeness of the glory* of the Lord' (Ezekiel 1:28). Isaiah's point is that a sinful person cannot survive the pure sight of God. Language has to be analogical or figurative in such situations.

A similarly vivid narrative tells how the Israelites begged Moses to tell them what God had said and not to put them in contact with God directly 'lest they die' (Exodus 20:18–20). Moses tells them that they should not fear, for God has come to test them and to put fear into them 'so that they should not sin'. Putting the fear of God into people has little support today—though the threat of prison or a horrible death for drink-driving seems to be OK! But is there still a case for true and loving *religious* deterrents—genuine warnings—without their becoming manipulative threats?

FOR REFLECTION

In what sense, if any, do any people of faith 'stand closer' to God than others and protect others from the wrath of God?

LEVITES *for* FIRSTBORN

Only Levites to be priests

This chapter presents some fascinating questions. It starts with the lineage of Aaron and Moses. Aaron's sons who continued to act as priests were Eleazar and Ithamar. Their elder brothers were Nadab and Abihu, who died as we saw in Leviticus 10, without children. This was a terrible fate for anyone in ancient Israel, especially since Nadab was Aaron's firstborn. There is apparently no embarrassment about this severe punishment, for it is mentioned again, and a further warning is given in verses 5–10. Only Aaron's descendants are to minister as priests. Outsiders, even Levitical non-Aaronites, are to be put to death if they presume to act as priest (vv. 10, 38). Samuel, born to Elkanah who was from Ephraim and the descendant of 'Zuph, an Ephraimite' according to 1 Samuel 1:1, is *apparently* given a Levitical pedigree in the genealogy in 1 Chronicles 6:1–29. Perhaps, however, we should think of him as a special case, dedicated to God's service as a child and put into the charge of the priest Eli. We are in no doubt of the overall emphasis: no one has a natural right to approach God. As Christians, we may 'approach the throne of grace *with boldness*', but should still note warnings about the holiness and awesomeness of God (for example, Hebrews 4:12–13, 16; 10:26–31).

Verse 7 probably means, 'They shall stand guard for him [Aaron] and for the whole congregation' and the word 'service' probably signifies primarily *physical* work. Hence we should not think that 'service' is something entirely churchy or concerned with worship. Those today who 'do the flowers', clean the floor, dust the seats, polish the brass, are in the same line as the specially appointed Levites of ancient times. This work together with the 'leading of services' constitutes a unified 'divine service'. People constantly get too pseudo-spiritual a view of what God requires, undervaluing the ordinary acts of kindness that can bring harmony and encouragement to people and are an undeniable demonstration of God's love for people.

Verses 11–13 connect the death of the firstborn of Egypt with the Levites as substitutes for the firstborn of Israel. The sequence of thought is:

Stage 1: Death of Egyptian firstborn sons; Israelite firstborn are spared (via the Passover lamb—not mentioned) but are consecrated to God.

Stage 2: The Levites are consecrated to God and the other firstborn of Israel are redeemed or released from the special obligations of consecration.

Verses 14–37 go systematically through the descendants of Levi, namely Gershon, Kohath and Merari, and their clans; then these three individually. Readers interested in family trees should consult a detailed commentary and make use of a concordance.

Census thinking

We have now come across three different censuses commanded by God:

- The males able to fight (that is, between 20 and 60) from twelve tribes (Joseph divided into two; Levi omitted) (1:2–46).

- The Levites from one month old upward (vv. 15–38). The numbers given are Gershon: 7,500; Kohath: 8,600; Merari: 6,200 = 22,300. Note that this gives 300 too many, so probably the Septuagint (the ancient Greek version of the Old Testament) is right to give Kohath as 8,300 in verse 28.

- The firstborn of Israel from one month old upward (22,273) (vv. 40–43).

When David commanded a census (2 Samuel 24; 1 Chronicles 21), the hard man, Joab, realized that it was a mistake, probably motivated by pride: 'May the Lord your God increase the number of the people... But why does my lord the king want to do this?' (2 Samuel 24:3). Sometimes even very unlikely people see things about us that we can miss.

FOR FURTHER THOUGHT

Redemption is a concept that prepares the way for a Christian theology of the cross: 'When the fullness of time had come, God sent his Son... to redeem those who were under the law' (Galatians 4:4–5).

HEREDITARY DUTIES *of the* LEVITES

We continue with the bookkeeping—more censuses, but this time the people numbered, all Levites, are aged 30 to 50, and their duties are to do with worship and not fighting. See comment on chapter 8 (pp. 124–125) for a different age range, 25 to 50.

The table of results is:

Clan	Verses	Duties	Number
Kohath	1–20, 34–37	Aaron and descendants cover up the holy things. The others carry them without touching them.	2750
Gershon	21–28, 38–41	Carry the curtains, hangings, and cords.	2630
Merari	29–33, 42–45	Carry the frames, pillars, bases, bars, pegs and cords.	3200
Total	46–49		8580

Again we note that the numbers are very high: I don't think I could visualize more than 8000 men working on a tent—even a large marquee. The figure of 580 *might* give a more realistic total number.

Official duties for twenty years

It is interesting to note that the 'working life' was from 30 to 50 for priests. We tend to regard 30 as past the prime of life for many professions (sport and high-stress occupations) but there is evidence that the Israelites, and others in the ancient world, thought that this was the age of maturity. Two 11th-century rabbis, Rashi and Ibn Ezra, regarded 30–50 as the age when physical strength was at its prime, and the Levites' chief duties consisted of carrying parts of the tabernacle. In a priest, what would be valued would be wisdom and experience, and stability. It seems likely that Ezekiel received his call to be a prophet 'in the thirtieth year' of his life (Ezekiel 1:1). At the upper limit, it is likely that many 50-year-old Israelites would seem to us to be much older, and certainly closer to a suitable retirement age. Despite the great ages attributed to Moses and others, the normal lifespan would have been much shorter than that in the West (or 'the North') today.

Other jobs for the Levites

It was not, of course, intended that Levites sat twiddling their thumbs until they were thirty years old. They would have needed some training beforehand. There would be work to do—they had fields, as we shall see, and they would need to be educated beyond the general level of the people. We know that, later on in Israel's history, the Levites had an important teaching function.

The motives behind the careful distribution of (hereditary) duties are not given, but they might have been to prevent quarrelling over the various duties—to do or to avoid doing—from self-importance or laziness, in an area where it was important to maintain a right attitude and focus. The Kohathites, the family of the Levites to which Aaron belonged, are told that they must not touch the holy things or they will die (v. 15). There is a subgroup within Kohath, however, who are assigned the special further task of allotting duties to the rest of the tribe (v. 19) in connection with 'the most holy things'—that is, those things within the 'holy of holies' or 'most holy place', notably the ark of the covenant. In doing this job conscientiously, Aaron will be saving the clans of the Kohathites from being destroyed (v. 17).

FOR REFLECTION

What would it have been like to be a Levite with the honour of carrying the tabernacle? Is it possible to regard a humping and carrying job as a privilege over a long period of time?

WIVES ON TRIAL

Our title today could have come from a tabloid newspaper, but the content of the chapter asks for it. A man who suspects his wife of adultery may require her to drink some unpleasant water and pronounce a curse upon herself. A woman who suspects her husband of adultery has no such recourse to the law. In fact, a married man who has intercourse with an unmarried and unengaged woman commits fornication, not adultery. The penalty for this was to marry the other woman—in addition to the wife or wives he already had. Even if this is acknowledged to be some sort of retribution for and deterrent against such behaviour, it was in no way a comfort to his existing wife!

God holding back?

We have seen, both in the study of Old Testament and in Church history, that God is rather non-directive in many ways. Certain Old Testament laws can be 'improved upon' by careful thought and experience, as well as by giving attention to New Testament teaching. So let's imagine the situation of Israel of old—patriarchal society and women with little *direct* power. It was accepted that a man could have more than one wife but that a woman could not have more than one husband, and might have to be satisfied with a half or less. Adultery was regarded as a capital offence, which was no doubt partly to do with inheritance: a woman always knows who her children are but a man does not. The sort of events set off by jealousy and suspicion have been dramatized many times and the result can be bitterness, ongoing recrimination, and even murder. So here is a way of settling the matter, laid down in the law and acceptable to the majority—presumably. There is a procedure that men are required to follow, which gives men a challenge and an opportunity. The woman risks pain and ostracism (v. 27) but has the opportunity to be vindicated and cleared of suspicion. The man risks public humiliation, for we can imagine what sort of looks he would get and remarks he would hear. The procedure would not be resorted to too enthusiastically. Instead people would be likely to sort things out privately.

If a woman went through the procedure without ill effects, the husband would be obliged to treat her properly—as innocent of any offence. A promise is given that she 'will be able to conceive children' (v. 28). If she proves to be guilty she becomes 'an execration' (v. 27). This was taken to mean that people would use her name as part of a curse: 'May you be cursed like N.' There is no requirement that she should be stoned. Was it that God would deal with her—as God had revealed the fault?

God intervening?

I wonder what part autosuggestion might have played in this procedure. Was it like a primitive lie detector? Or does God actually undertake to intervene and give a demonstration of justice? It seems very rare for this sort of thing to happen, and I have not come across comparable procedures today (although they may exist). It seems to me that God does not undertake to act in regularly interventionist ways that can be guaranteed. The nearest I have heard of was from a young woman who spent time with Jackie Pullinger-To in Hong Kong and was involved in praying with people coming off heroin by means of 'cold turkey' (that is, without the aid of other drugs). She said that she had never seen anyone, during the course of a whole year, go through the frightening and distressing physical experiences that usually accompany this process.

Certainly, in the Old Testament, people expected God to intervene in the practice of drawing lots, and in the use of Urim and Thummim. We do not know how these methods were carried out but it is clear that they were used regularly in the early part of Israel's history. God's will was sought by these means and believed to be obtained. Samuel and Elisha are examples of prophets who were known to have clairvoyant powers (1 Samuel 9:6–9; 2 Kings 4:27). In 2 Kings 4, Elisha regards it as unusual that he does not know the cause of the woman's distress.

This raises the important question of whether we have lost something that God intended us to keep, as many charismatic Christians would maintain, or whether we have 'progressed' beyond these primitive times. Are the gifts of the Spirit meant to be the norm today, including 'words of knowledge'?

FOR REFLECTION

Have we actually progressed from the Numbers 5 situation in terms of trusting God and in dealing fairly with marital conflict?

NAZIRITES, *the* HAIRY HOLY ONES

There is a natural assumption, confirmed by many scholars, that Nazirites took lifelong vows and that Samson and possibly Samuel were typical Nazirites. Samuel is, in fact, called a Nazirite in 1 Samuel 1:22, but only in one of the manuscripts of the Dead Sea Scrolls. Neither the Hebrew nor any of the ancient versions of the Old Testament contain this reference. Moreover, Numbers 6 does not envisage lifelong vows as the norm (see vv. 9–12). The phrases 'all the days of their nazirite vow', 'all the days they separate themselves to the Lord', 'all their days as Nazirites' and so on (vv. 5, 6, 8) imply that the vows applied for a set and limited period. Verses 9–12 evidently have in mind a situation where a Nazirite accidentally breaks the conditions by touching a dead body and has to start the vow again (vv. 9, 12b). I wonder if Samson managed not to touch anyone after he killed them! Or was war an unstated but understood exception to the rule?

The regulations

Nazirite regulations covered diet (no grape products, vv. 3–4), hair (no shaving at all, v. 5) and corpses (no touching, even of close relatives, vv. 6–8). If a Nazirite did touch a corpse, because of a sudden death or other reason, then their head was defiled. They ceased to be a Nazirite, and had to shave their head, offer sacrifices (two doves or pigeons, as sin offering and burnt offering, and one male lamb), and start again (vv. 9–12).

After the time of consecration they were to offer two yearling lambs (male for a burnt offering, female for a sin offering), and a ram as a peace offering (plus unleavened bread, a drink offering and cereal offering). The peace offering was eaten by the worshipper and the priests.

Vows then and now

The Hebrew root n-z-r from which the word 'Nazirite' comes has the basic meanings of 'dedicate, consecrate, separate', and the word 'holiness' has a similar basic meaning. The idea of 'being separate for God' finds expression in all sorts of cultures throughout history. Most religions have a category of 'priest' or something similar, setting those persons apart from other human beings. The Old Testament makes the point with respect to the tribe of Levi, which is set apart to perform the priestly rites of Israel. The Nazirite is essentially an expression of a time of special dedication to God, a time of more concentrated focus upon serving God, a time when special and particular vows might be made—not always wisely (see below). Refraining from alcohol (and grape products—perhaps potential alcohol—there were no sell-by dates in those times) seems to be a sign of turning deliberately away from earthly pleasure, but it may also allude to the loss of control that alcohol can bring and which is severely condemned in the Bible. Not cutting off the hair may signify renunciation of vanity and pride in appearance, though there is no absolute prohibition against trimming the hair.

As we have seen previously, the laws of the Old Testament, though extensive, are not exhaustive and do not cater for every possible situation. What should happen, for example, when someone makes a vow that is foolish? Jephthah and his daughter assumed that it had to be honoured but the narrator makes no comment (Judges 11:30, 34–35). When Saul made a foolish vow, requiring the death of his son Jonathan, the people 'ransomed' him (1 Samuel 14:24, 43–45). The text seems to mean that they simply stood with Jonathan and rejected the vow, arguing that God had been with him and would continue to be. Scholars have *conjectured*—no more than this—that they might have ransomed him by paying money, or sacrificing an animal.

Since the principle of 'redemption' or 'substitution' has a good pedigree, perhaps it is applicable to vows? One might replace a foolish vow, or one simply designed to make life difficult (as if God has pleasure in that), by one that has useful service as its goal.

FOR MEDITATION

Monks and nuns today make lifelong vows, typically of poverty, chastity and obedience. Great care is taken, over a period of years of testing, to make sure that the person making the vow has thought through the implications of it and is making it for the right reasons. What are the vows you have made during the course of your Christian life (such as baptism, confirmation, covenant service, prayer of commitment)? How are you doing?

The AARONIC BLESSING

Today's short reading contains the lovely prayer of blessing that is used in liturgies all over the world, and which has been set to music many times. John Rutter's 'The Lord bless you and keep you' has become very popular in recent years, and rightly so, for here we meet some supremely significant words and concepts.

Blessing

'Blessing' is one of those words that is used widely and with a variety of meanings—mostly vague. 'Bless you' after an act of kindness means, more or less, 'thanks'; after a sneeze it means just about nothing at all (although it originally expressed a prayer that the sneezer didn't have the plague). 'God bless' seems to be the equivalent of 'Have a nice day'. 'God bless you' *might* be a prayer for the addressee's well-being. In the Old Testament the word is similarly flexible. The exchange in Ruth 2:4 between Boaz and his reapers seems to be quite conventional: 'The Lord be with you'—'The Lord bless you'. No doubt, however, it has more depth than 'How do you do'—'How do you do' (no question marks needed).

The word comes from a root that means either 'kneel' or 'bless'. There may be an explanation here of the fact that people are said to 'bless God', as in Genesis 24:48: 'I bowed my head and worshipped the Lord... and blessed the Lord... who had led me...'. A person would kneel to receive a blessing (from God's representative) and also to praise or worship God. 'Blessed be the name of the Lord' (Job 1:21) is a frequent prayer in the Old Testament.

The significant theological meaning can be understood by looking at the importance given to the pronouncement of a blessing by a father just before his death (see Jacob and Esau, Genesis 27:26ff; Jacob and his sons, Genesis 49:1–28). A word spoken out loud puts into effect a commitment to what is said. A word spoken out loud cannot be taken back (compare Judges 11:35 and Isaiah 55:11). Even today, in our very different culture, we know something of the feeling of decision and clarity that comes from putting one's hazy thoughts into definite speech. As many (including Winnie the Pooh) have said, 'I don't know what I think until I say it.' As with a spoken absolution, the priestly blessing is a confirmation to the senses, and thereby the inner person, that God is actually disposed in such a way towards the worshipper. So verse 27 describes the result of this blessing: the name of Yahweh is upon the people, marking them out as his own, *and he will bless them*.

God is the source of all blessing and this is emphasized here, where the special covenant name 'Yahweh' (see Exodus 6:2–8) occurs not once (which would have been grammatically sufficient) but three times. Certain individual human beings have the privilege and responsibility of pronouncing blessing in God's name. As well as the priest and heads of families, others in the Old Testament pronounce blessing—for example, Joshua upon Caleb, either as his leader or his father-in-law (Joshua 14;13), and David, as king, upon Barzillai (2 Samuel 19:39).

The words in the remainder of verses 24–26 produce a cumulative effect: 'keep you' (see the emphasis on this word in Psalm 121:3, 4, 5, 7, 8), 'make his face shine upon you', 'lift up his countenance upon you', 'be gracious', 'give you peace'. As with many words, the aim is not to have one precise meaning but to produce many resonances. The sun shines (literally 'causes to be or become light') and dispels the darkness of the night, with its dangers and confusion. A lamp shines similarly.

Peace

The Hebrew for 'peace' is well known: *shalom* (compare the Arabic *salaam*. The name 'Solomon' is from this root). As with all words, continual use can water down its content (compare 'absolutely lethal', meaning 'pretty bad') and, as with 'blessed', it is used as a conventional greeting. Used in significant contexts, however, it implies wholeness, health of body, mind and spirit, and good relationships— a peace that actually meets and overcomes hatred and strife. Jesus promised this peace to his followers. Have a look through a concordance some time and see how both 'bless(ing)' and 'peace' are used in the Bible.

FOR MEDITATION AND ACTION

'Bless those who curse you, pray for those who abuse you.'

Luke 6:28

ISRAEL'S HOLY DESERT WAGONS

It's difficult to avoid thinking of old Western films when reading this chapter—wagons setting out into the vast, arid unknown to look for a place to settle, having to defend themselves against attacks from Indians from time to time. The picture here is actually very different. Most of the people of Israel were on foot—at least, we assume so. The wagons, each drawn by two oxen and not horses, were only six in number and were for the purpose of carrying 'holy things' such as the curtains and poles that made up the tent of meeting. The 'most holy things' were to be carried on the shoulders (v. 9, and see 4:5–15). A clay model of a wagon with a rounded top, dating from about 2500BC, has been found, so perhaps we are not so far out with the wild west comparison. Two-wheeled wagons seem to have been more popular later on.

When we ask where the wagons came from, and about the expertise to make them, we have few firm answers. Certainly there were resources available to the Israelites that the Bible is not concerned to tell us. They overcame several hostile tribes *en route* and had the opportunity to take both 'precious items' and practical things. So perhaps we should think of the six wagons as part of a larger stock, officially given to the Levites at this point in the journey. It seems that the Bible allows for artistic variation in the way details are presented.

The purpose of the regulations

More important is the purpose for which this story is told. Emphases that stand out clearly are:

- the central place of the tribe of Levi in carrying out sacred ritual duties
- the holiness of anything directly connected with the Lord
- the equal participation of all the twelve tribes (Jacob's twelve sons, minus Levi, with Joseph divided into two) in public worship, which defined Israel's existence; irrespective of size, each tribe brings the same offerings
- the necessity of approaching the Lord on his own terms, as he himself directs

- the value of lavish generosity in our service of God. (Note the silver and gold in each offering. It is difficult to be sure of the equivalent of one shekel, but it may well be about 11.4 g or 0.4 oz. 130 shekels = 3 lb 4 oz, or nearly 1.5 kg.)

The events described here took place during the same period as those described from Exodus 40:2 onwards, the first to the twelfth of the first month of the second year. The 'cart a day' sequence is described here in more detail. The wagon distribution (each with two oxen) is: Gershonites 2, Merarites 4, Kohathites 0 (see Numbers 4 for details of their several responsibilities). To me, this sounds very hard on the Kohathites (I hate trekking, even with a small rucksack), but it was a special honour to carry the most holy things. Those who have seen the Good Friday processions in Spain, where heavy images of Christ, Mary and so on are carried for hours on end on men's shoulders, will not find this surprising.

The idea of consecration of objects is common in the Old Testament. The tabernacle (*mishkan*) and the altar are also said to be 'anointed', which is common for prophets, priests and kings (and a few other people) but rare for objects. Certain items could be consecrated to the service of God alone. So it was a great abomination when Belshazzar the Babylonian king allowed his guests to drink from the sacred vessels (Daniel 5:3; William Walton catches something of the horror of this act in his *Belshazzar's Feast*). This feeling is still around—the silver chalice for Holy Communion is not used for any other purpose—and yet, for many, there is a feeling of uneasiness. Should we not have got beyond this by now? The temple has gone and we may worship God anywhere 'in spirit and in truth' through the Holy Spirit (John 4:24). Things set aside may indeed serve an important purpose—as a symbol or reminder, for example. The main problems come, now as always, when the practice is misused and superstition creeps in, or a religious practice is used to avoid a human duty (compare Mark 7).

PRAYER

O invisible God, thank you for our place of worship
and its holy symbols. May they always point beyond themselves
to you, the only true God.

The GIFT of the LEVITES

The Levites are first of all regarded as the substitute sacrifice for the firstborn of the rest of Israel. They belong to God but their lives are not forfeit. Instead he 'gives them unreservedly as a gift to Aaron and his descendants' (vv. 16, 19), possibly a strange concept which deliberately reminds us of slavery. However, this is slavery with privilege (compare also Ephesians 6:6: 'slaves of Christ, doing the will of God from the heart').

The regulations

The Levites are allowed here to officiate for 25 years maximum (vv. 23–26). This conflicts with Numbers 4, where Levitical service was permitted from the age of 30, rather than 25. Possibly, there was a change in the regulations due to different circumstances from time to time (1 Chronicles 23:24, 27; 2 Chronicles 31:17 and Ezra 3:8 have 20 as the lower limit and no upper age limit). The regulations require retirement at a fixed point but give freedom to 'assist' after that—perhaps especially in a non-stipendiary capacity.

This section really begins at 7:89, with the note about how Moses received instruction from the Lord in the tent of meeting. The voice came from above the ark of the covenant, specifically from above the *kapporeth* which was on the top of the ark. The word may mean 'cover' or—since it is from the same root as 'atone' (compare *Yom Kippur*)—'mercy seat'. Even Moses was not allowed within the holy of holies, so he presumably heard from outside the curtain.

The first instructions concern the seven-branched lampstand, the *menorah* (Exodus 25:31–40), the term used later of the eight-branched candlestick used in the festival of Hanukkah. The light is to shine in front of the lampstand—towards the people. The significance is probably that God's light shines on his people (compare the Aaronic blessing that we saw at the end of Numbers 6). The lamp would have had to be tended morning and evening.

A double substitution

The bulk of the chapter gives the regulations for setting aside the Levites. After the prescribed washings:

- The people (probably their representatives only) lay their hands on the heads of the Levites (v. 10). The Levites will henceforth be acting for the people.

- The Levites lay their hands on two young bulls (v. 12). The bulls will be 'acting for' the Levites. Aaron presents one as a sin offering and one a burnt offering (plus their cereal offerings).

The whole operation, therefore, represents a double substitution. The bulls are sacrificed—offered up—instead of the Levites, who were offered up instead of the firstborn of Israel.

The Passover was the time when the firstborn of Egypt died, but the firstborn of Israel escaped by means of the Passover Lamb. Its blood was smeared on the doorposts and lintel as a sign to 'the destroyer' not to enter the house to strike dead the firstborn. Associated with this, in Exodus 13:1–16, is the teaching that all firstborn, animals and humans, belong to the Lord. The clean animals must be sacrificed to God; unclean animals may not be sacrificed but can either be killed (by breaking the neck, that is, not as a sacrifice) or redeemed with a sheep (v. 13). Children must be redeemed, and this law is to be kept strictly so as to provide a teaching aid for future generations. When the child asks what it means, the parent is to tell the story of the liberation from Egypt (vv. 14–16). Among Orthodox Jews today, all firstborn males are instructed to fast on the eve of Pesach (Passover).

Great stress was laid on the importance of the firstborn son in Israel. They inherited a double portion and could not be disinherited (Deuteronomy 21:15–17). This throws light on the meaning of New Testament references to Christ, who is the firstborn among many brothers and sisters (Romans 8:29), the firstborn of Mary (Matthew 1:25; Luke 2:7), the firstborn from the dead (Colossians 1:18) and even the firstborn of all creation (Colossians 1:15). As a result of belonging to him, we ourselves belong to 'the assembly of the firstborn' (Hebrews 12:23).

PRAYER

Christ, our Passover Lamb, our elder brother, our great high priest, we thank you for the priestly privilege we have of presenting our own selves as a living sacrifice (Romans 12:1).

The PASSOVER: BETTER LATE *than* NEVER: FOLLOW THAT CLOUD

More guidance needed

What to do when the regulations don't fit? This must have been a bigger problem than we might realize from an unimaginative reading of Old Testament law. The problem has bothered religious people through the ages and they have come up with all sorts of solutions. The Puritans noted that organs are not expressly allowed in the Bible and so forbade them. Others argued that organs were not expressly forbidden and so allowed them.

New laws for new situations

Joshua wrote statutes and ordinances in the book of the law of God (Joshua 24:25–26), yet there is no section of the Pentateuch headed 'Joshua's Supplement'. This represents one way of dealing with new situations: to work out (with careful thought and prayer, we hope) how the principles already accepted would apply. The decision is noted and has recognized authority. Today, of course, we have no possibility of adding to the Bible in order to cope with, for example, human cloning, international debt, submission to foreign law or pornography on the internet, but we do have biblical principles and analogies to guide us. Decisions reached are enshrined in law, whether national, international, church or local council, and must be obeyed. The resources available include our experience, traditions (civil and religious), knowledge (scientific, psychological, medical, sociological and common sense). But the incident in Numbers 9:8–14 shows a different way—a direct answer from God.

Direct divine guidance

Most of the alleged divine answers that I have come across have been either quite trivial or curiously unconvincing. It is not surprising that there are disputes when the attraction of clarity or even certainty meets with a scepticism born of experience and even disillusionment. Nevertheless, the pattern presented here reminds us that we believe in a *living God* who has given us his Holy Spirit to 'lead us into all truth' (John 14:16–17; 16:13). There is no need to belittle the importance of the God-given resources listed above, in order to give an important place to prayer and waiting upon God, as Moses did. In a mysterious way, Moses spoke to God face to face (12:7–8; but compare also Exodus 33:21–23), whereas we see 'in a glass darkly' (1 Corinthians 13:12; you would need to have a look at an ancient mirror to get an approximation to Paul's meaning. Glass was not available till late Roman times—and then not the regular glass that we know).

Community is vital

The decision Moses came up with was one that we might possibly have guessed: if you can't manage the date set, keep the Passover exactly one month later (v. 11). (Ah, but what if you miss the second one too?) The strictness of the judgment is surprising: keep it or be cut off from your people (v. 13). The communal festivals of Israel were a vital sign of the solidarity of all God's people, a recognition of their dependence on him for their very existence, an expression of their commitment to continue to walk in his ways. Our society is much more individualistic than ancient Israel's, and there is a certain acknowledgment in the Old Testament that this development has a good side (Jeremiah 31:29–30; Ezekiel 18:2). However, there is also a loss, and the gradual move into services on TV, drive-in services and even cyber-religion has almost certainly led to a weakening of personal relationships and community which are the essence of the Church.

The cloud that guided them by day and the fire that assured them by night (v. 16) were important signs for the people of Israel. I wonder how easy they were to see—how recognizable. Elijah's servant had to look very hard (and seven times) to see the cloud like a person's hand (1 Kings 18:44). Whatever it was like for them, many failed to be reassured. We ourselves are not promised unmistakable signs, but we are enjoined to watch steadfastly, and by faith, to discern the signs of God's presence and activity.

FOR REFLECTION

God's grace is not always obvious, but it is sufficient (2 Corinthians 12:9). Is this your experience? How can we be alongside those who do not find it to be so?

DEPARTURE *from* SINAI

Authorized trumpets

Now why would you need to have *divine* laws about blowing a trumpet? The code is also laid down by God:

- One blast to assemble the leaders and head of tribes (v. 4)
- Two blasts to assemble all the people (v. 3)
- One alarm call (music not specified—presumably they had a traditional alarm call): tribes on the east set out (v. 5)
- Two alarm calls: tribes on the south set out (v. 6)
- Presumably three and four calls indicate that west and north respectively are to set out

This seems like the sort of agreement that could be written down in council bye-laws, and to have them enshrined in the book of the law of God seems heavy, but perhaps we can at least understand some of the advantages. It would give the sort of authority necessary to prevent chaos in times of danger, when people would be frightened and tempted to see to their own interests and forget discipline. Most of all, it would give the assurance that God hears and remembers his people (vv. 9–10). Although these verses suggest that the trumpet will be a reminder *to God* (which he does not logically need), this statement is made so that the Israelites might have the assurance that God hears. The trumpet alarm call would, in effect, be a sacrament. Actually, verse 10 gives us new and surprising information. At least, in reading through the regulations about sacrifices, I personally had not imagined the sort of loud trumpet-accompanied rejoicing indicated here. And here, there does seem to be scope for improvization. This is a further reminder that Western restraint is not God's ideal for all occasions.

The journey continues

Verses 11 onward describe the start of the next phase of the journey, beginning on the twentieth day of the second month of the second year after they came out of Egypt. This is the first time the Israelites have moved on since Exodus 19! The order of marching is specified:

- Judah, Issachar and Zebulun
- Merari and Gershon (to set up the tabernacle)
- Reuben, Simeon and Gad
- Kohath (with the holy things to put in the tabernacle)
- Ephraim, Manasseh and Benjamin (the Rachel tribes)
- Dan, Asher and Naphtali

Fellow travellers in faith

The phrase 'Hobab son of Reuel the Midianite, Moses' father-in-law' (v. 29) leaves us uncertain as to whether Hobab was actually the father-in-law or his son. On the other hand, Exodus 2:18 refers to Moses' father-in-law himself as Reuel, and in Exodus 18:27 his father-in-law goes back to Midian. It is often the case in reading the Bible that we cannot be sure of the exact meaning of a passage. It is clear, however, that we do know *some* things. Hobab was a Midianite whose knowledge of the desert was especially valuable. Whether the same as or different from Hobab, Jethro = Reuel = Moses' father-in-law, a priest of Midian, had (also) been of immense help. His advice had stimulated Moses into setting up a pattern of delegation (or perhaps two-tier expertise) and thus preserving his health and sanity (Exodus 18:13–27). There is a very open sort of attitude displayed here, somewhat reminiscent of the situation in the book of Genesis. There we find Abraham and his descendants wandering freely among the Canaanites, setting up altars, relating naturally and without religious aggression to Melchizedek. Sometimes Christians have assumed that all who fail to express definite faith in Christ, or who actually belong to other religions, are in some way hostile to the Christian faith. This has prevented a respectful and loving evangelism which gives people the benefit of the doubt. Moses' low-key evangelistic message (though he wouldn't have called it that) is, 'Join us. The Lord will bless you as he will bless us' (v. 32).

The ark was carried before the Israelites as an effective sign—a sacrament, again—of God's presence with them. We know from the story of the Philistines in 1 Samuel 4:1–11 that it did not guarantee victory. There is a vast difference between a sacrament and a magic charm. It was both an encouragement and a challenge.

FOR MEDITATION

Since God is with us, we may go forth in this dangerous desert with boldness. Since God is with us, we must act as his holy people.

'BURNING' & 'CRAVING-GRAVES'

There's complaining and complaining

The book of Numbers contains accounts of eight separate rebellious complainings, and here we read of the first two. Verses 1–3 tell us in summary fashion of complaining 'in the hearing of the Lord'. This is a puzzling phrase since it is impossible to say or even think anything that the Lord cannot detect. The Old Testament itself makes this point in certain places (for example, Psalm 139:4), so do we simply have a primitive and naive strand here? Rather, I think, the phrase signifies either a deliberate intention that the Lord should hear, or at least not caring that he hears. It's rather like composing a letter and deliberating over whether to send it or not. Sometimes you decide, 'Yes, I *will* send this critical letter'; sometimes you say, 'Well, I'll take a chance on it and let it go.' One of our problems in the analogy is, of course, that God is present when we are thinking out what we want to say to him. However, it may be helpful, and true, to imagine God as giving us space to think things through—perhaps to allow us to go to our own room free from parental interference. The Israelites almost certainly did a great deal of moaning, as many of us do today (even if you, dear reader, do not). What is signified here is a deliberate challenging of God's dealings with the people, and it was punished by fire, hence the name of the place 'Taberah' or 'Burning'. The word is often used figuratively (for example, the 'burning' snakes in ch. 21) so it is not clear exactly what sort of judgment is signified: possibly some tents literally caught fire, possibly it was some sort of burning fever. Whatever it was, the people asked their mediator Moses to pray for them and God heard their cry. This is the 'last word' of the story—grace and not judgment.

Selective memory

The task of mediating between God and these fickle people is a great burden. The privilege of having access to God to pray today on behalf of others is also very taxing. The next rebellion drives even Moses to the edge. He has recently been portrayed as assuring Hobab that the Lord will do Israel good, but here he complains to the Lord in almost blasphemous terms, or so it seems (vv. 11–15). The problem is that the people are getting fed up with manna and are looking back with rose-tinted spectacles to the time in Egypt. Perhaps the 'rabble' (v. 4) are the non-Israelites who may have had a better life in Egypt, and who left because they recognized *at the time* the reality of the Lord's power. Either way, the majority of the people have forgotten the bad things, including their oppression, the impossible demands laid on them by their slave-drivers and the many deaths that must have resulted from this. Also, they filter out the good things and magnify them: 'Do you remember how we used to catch fish—we didn't have to pay for it—when we were in Egypt? It was delicious, wasn't it? Now it's manna morning, noon and night' (vv. 5–6). Of course, this behaviour is all too understandable, but it is not condonable. Nevertheless, the Lord knows and understands the hardships that we go through. It is possible to 'share them with God' without adopting a rebellious attitude, and ask him to give us endurance and grateful hearts.

Well, you asked for it

The result of this rebellion was that God gave them what they asked for—meat in the form of quails—and something extra—a plague. This causes problems to the Christian theologian for it seems that God is acting petulantly and vindictively. Clearly it must be read in the light of what we believe about 'the God and Father of our Lord Jesus Christ' who 'so loved us that he gave his only begotten Son' (1 Peter 1:3; John 3:16). The passage then gives us a timely warning about pushing for our own agenda rather than seeking to understand what God's plans are. Compare the warnings about making your own light, in Isaiah 50:10–11. It may be that there are natural explanations to place alongside the theological account given in the text—for example, the meat was kept too long (it passed its drop-and-eat-by date?) and caused food poisoning. Perhaps there is an added boost for vegetarianism in the desert. The main point is unaffected by these speculations, however. The only safe way forward, for body and soul, is to follow God's plans. The grisly name Kibroth-hattaavah (Graves of Craving) would be a reminder to future generations.

FOR REFLECTION

'If you don't change "Xmas" to "Christmas" in the minutes, I'll raise merry hell at the church council meeting' (from an actual telephone conversation). How pleased might God be with such zeal?

SPIRIT-FILLED ASSISTANTS

Dealing gently with rash words

Moses' complaint to God binds together two separate incidents, or, to put it another way, produces a double response from God. 'You complain, Moses, that you can't cope with this nation of grumblers? OK, I will teach both you and them a lesson about my ability to provide— and perhaps you will all realize in future that, if I decide to give a specific gift, there's a good reason for it. And I will also provide help for you, Moses, in leading the people' (vv. 16–23).

A word first about Moses' prayer. He is angry. He speaks with biting sarcasm. What he says is not a model for those learning to pray. Yet there is a world of difference between this prayer, the prayer of a desperate man who takes his life in his hands, and the sort of familiar, cheeky prayers that are sometimes heard at prayer meetings. And the Lord knows the difference. Compare with this the anguished prayers of Job (7; 10; 14) and Jeremiah (20:7–10). God even deals gently and graciously with the unreasonable Jonah (4:1–10). Note also that Moses addresses God directly rather than grumbling 'behind his back'. There is only the merest hint of a rebuke to Moses in verse 23. God understands this man with whom he speaks face to face. He encourages honesty and the outpouring of those deep feelings that come from the frustrations of obedience.

The nature of the Spirit

The story of how the Spirit came upon the seventy elders (vv. 24–25) is another puzzling passage. The New Testament teaches, especially in John (see 14:25–26; 15:26–27; 16:12–15), that the Holy Spirit is *personal*, and certainly not a substance to be dolloped out, as we might assume simply from Numbers 11:17. Both Testaments, however, tell of the Lord's 'pouring out his Spirit' and we must take the different types of imagery as contributing to a complex reality ultimately beyond our understanding. We are, after all, speaking of God the Holy Spirit. This seems to be figurative language, accommodating to limited human understanding, which asserts the unity of the spirit experienced by Moses and the elders. The elders are anointed with the Spirit in order to share the spiritual ministry of Moses. We are not told why neither the elders appointed in Exodus 18:25–26 nor the priests could support Moses in the way that he needed, but clearly these newly appointed men supply what they could not.

Prophecy of various kinds

The actual 'prophesying' of the elders seems to be like that of Saul in 1 Samuel 10:5–13, when no prophetic message seems to have been given but he was 'changed into a different person'. Clearly there was some visible sign to the people that 'the spirit rested upon them' (v. 26). Perhaps there is some sort of parallel with speaking in tongues, where the speaker is unaware of what he or she is saying. Moreover, just as Paul pronounces 'prophecy' to be a higher gift than speaking in tongues (1 Corinthians 14:5), so the ideal of Old Testament prophecy is to speak with God and understand clearly what he says (as we shall see clearly in the next chapter). Thus both Testaments offer a stimulus to Christians that is both positive and negative: don't despise the basic forms of the gifts of the Spirit, but press on to know God more and more.

There is a further instructive twist to the story, in that 68 elders receive the spirit in the tent of meeting, but two of them, Eldad and Medad, are out among the people in the camp. They also prophesy in full view (vv. 26–27). Joshua is afraid that they might usurp Moses' authority in being seen so openly to be authorized by God, and wants Moses to stop them. Moses' reply (v. 29) has many reverberations.

- In the new era of the Spirit, the Lord will pour out his Spirit on all flesh (Joel 2:28, quoted by Peter in Acts 2)—a contrast with the limited group of elders who prophesied once only (v. 25).

- Paul rejoiced that the gospel was preached even by people antagonistic towards him (Philippians 1:15–18) and also said to the Corinthians, 'I would like all of you to speak in tongues, but even more to prophesy' (1 Corinthians 14:5).

- Jesus told the disciples not to stop others from casting out demons in his name, for 'whoever is not against us is for us' (Mark 9:39–40).

FOR REFLECTION

'Is the Lord's power limited? Now you shall see…' (v. 23). Is there anything at present that God is prompting you to ask of him, that only he can bring about?

HOW COME YOU WERE NOT AFRAID?

The Lord's words to Aaron and Miriam in verse 8 should bring us up sharply whenever we are tempted to criticize our leaders. They are authorized by God and need to be respected. Moses was an outstanding leader with an especially close relationship to God, so his critics were likely to be straying on to dangerous ground. Let's try to understand the nature of the comments made by Aaron and Miriam, Moses' brother and sister.

Certainly Moses was not beyond reproach, and many of our leaders have faults that are much more obvious. There is nothing wrong with loyal and constructive criticism. For good examples of this in the Old Testament, see Jethro's advice to Moses and Joab's (rather more forceful) advice to David (Exodus 18:17–18; 2 Samuel 19:5–8; 24:3—I have a soft spot for the hard man, Joab). But the New Testament is insistent that it is God's intention that we should submit to both civil and religious leaders. When Paul was provoked into retorting, 'God will strike you, you whitewashed wall...' (Acts 23:3), he apologized when he discovered that he was speaking to the high priest, even though the latter was clearly in the wrong, and he quoted Exodus 22:28, 'You shall not speak evil of a leader of your people'. Paul even commands obedience to the Roman government, which was often far from just and benign (Romans 13:1–7; Titus 3:1; 1 Peter 2:13).

Marrying out

What of the fact that Moses had married a Cushite woman? (v. 1). There is a fair sprinkling of material about foreign marriages in the Old Testament. Abraham was concerned that Isaac should marry one of his own kindred and not a Canaanite woman (Genesis 24:2–4), although Abraham had come from a pagan background, so this might not signify a purely spiritual motivation—the characters in biblical narrative cannot always be *assumed* to be doing what is best. However, we do note the conviction that the Lord will guide (Genesis 24:7, 12–14, 21)—and that he did guide (Genesis 24:48, 50). Rebekah's motives in sending Jacob to get a wife from the home country were suspect, but she came up with a rationalization that appealed to Isaac

(Genesis 27:42–46). The perceived danger in marrying foreign women is that they will lead the people (via their husbands and children) away from worshipping the Lord, but women who trust him are welcomed (see especially Ruth and Rahab: Ruth 1:16–17; 2:12; 4:11–12; Joshua 6:25).

It may be that 'Cushite' is another name for 'Midianite', and that this woman is actually Zipporah, Jethro's daughter. This does seem an odd way of referring to her, however, and 'Cushite' usually means someone from Ethiopia.

Leaders with hidden agendas

Having leaders at loggerheads means that a vulnerable community may not survive. More serious still, the challenge to Moses was a challenge to God, as he was known by all to have had a divine call to lead the people. A similar challenge by an insignificant member of the people would have been less dangerous, but here visible and decisive action is needed and swiftly taken. We have noted other exceptional acts of judgment at critical times (the strange fire before the Lord and the blasphemer, Leviticus 10:1–2; 24:10–23) and this narrative serves as a serious warning for all who followed.

Was it male prejudice that Miriam and not Aaron should have been struck with leprosy? Perhaps the high priest is spared by reason of his office—if so, he has had a double let-off and should be doubly aware of his responsibilities afterwards. Aaron recognizes in verse 11 that both are under judgment: 'do not lay sin upon us'. He expresses his repentance and Moses, as previously, acts as mediator-intercessor. The seven days' delay laid down by God are to demonstrate the seriousness of the offence (v. 14).

In the current atmosphere, where it is customary to criticize, make jokes about, and even mock political leaders, it is hardly possible to recover the attitudes recommended here. Are our attitudes towards church and civil leaders in line with the message of this chapter?

FOR REFLECTION

I wonder what would be the result if a member of a church committee opposed the pastor or minister and was struck with leprosy. Why do we not generally think of it as a serious possibility?

55 NUMBERS 13

DIVINELY AUTHORIZED SPYING

Guarding the truth

I've often wondered what the world would be like without spies. Le Carré-type spying involves deception at the deepest possible level and all sorts of objectionable behaviour seems inevitably to follow. Winston Churchill said that in wartime the truth is so precious that it needs to be protected by a bodyguard of lies. The spying authorized in this chapter, of course, was much more straightforward—an assessment of the problem of invading, grasping the geography of the terrain, trying to form effective strategies. It required, as with the spies who visited Rahab in Jericho (Joshua 2), secrecy and deception in some form. There is no necessity for anyone to volunteer the whole truth in every situation and Jesus deliberately kept back certain facts in order not to overburden the disciples (John 16:12). But what if someone asks direct questions: Who are you? Where are you from? What is the purpose of your visit? The line between ethical reticence and actual lies is easily crossed. It seems that spying is one of those activities that belongs to a fallen world—as does war itself, of course. It *may* be necessary but should not become a way of life. God already knows more than any spy and can direct those who are in tune with him, which is, we hope, the aspiration of every Christian. We know of many incidents of divine warning and protection (in the Bible and in history) but also of mistakes made by people who *imagined* that they were in touch with God. There is no easy way forward but there is a way to be found.

Negative spin wins

One leader from each tribe was to go and investigate the land, no doubt to make clear that all would inherit and so that each could address his own tribe. (The route they took is shown on the map on p. 26.) The names of all the spies are recorded in verses 4–15, which is very unfortunate for those who simply went down in history as the ones who set back the conquest of Canaan by nearly forty years. Only Caleb and Joshua brought back an upbeat report: 'Yes, the land is great, and we can conquer it.' All twelve spies agreed with the first point, but ten of them estimated that the inhabitants were too strong and numerous, the cities too well-fortified, and populated all over by several tribes. Notice how the spies describe it in verse 27: admittedly it flows with milk and honey but it is not 'the land which he swore to our ancestors to give to them and to their descendants'. Rather, they employ the subtle phraseology, '…the land to which *you sent us*'.

Caleb's attempt to present a positive evaluation (v. 30) is met by an 'unfavourable report' (v. 32). The one Hebrew word translated by this phrase comes from a root meaning 'to glide or slide' and can mean a 'whispering, defamation or evil report'. It can mean a true report of bad circumstances, but here it seems to signify a false or misleading report. There certainly seems to be misrepresentation in saying that the land 'eats its inhabitants'—that is, that they perish (v. 32). Gordon Wenham suggests that the penalty for falsely accusing the land of murder is to undergo the death penalty (compare Deuteronomy 19:16–19). Perhaps, but the definite charge against the ten spies is that they have 'despised the Lord and refused to believe him', as we shall see in 14:11.

'Grasshoppers' (v. 33) is an obvious exaggeration, but what about the grapes? Children's Bibles sometimes have pictures of two men carrying on a pole a standard artist's triangular sort of bunch of grapes, with each grape the size of a football. Is that what's intended by the description in this chapter? It seems unlikely that this would have been imagined by later generations who actually lived in the land, but we can well visualize a large section of a vine which could conveniently be carried on a pole. The precise meaning of the word 'cluster' is uncertain, but this interpretation seems reasonable.

The famous Goliath may have been related to 'the Nephilim'. He was estimated to be over nine feet tall (1 Samuel 17:4)—comparable to the tallest man in *The Guinness Book of Records*.

It is often difficult to tell the difference between faith and foolishness, between a divine call to step out and an irresponsible risk, between waiting upon the Lord and taking decisive action. It is often difficult to judge whether godly dissatisfaction is called for, or humble acceptance of a situation. What guidelines might we suggest?

FOR REFLECTION

There's a lot in the Bible about the peace of God but nothing
positive about lethargy and inertia.

POWER *in* FORGIVENESS

The depth of Israel's disillusionment and her consequent rebellion goes deeper here than at any time previously. The people actually plan to replace God's divinely appointed and proven leader with someone who will take them back to Egypt. The threat to stone Caleb and Joshua (v. 10) recalls the penalty for true and courageous testimony to those who have no ears to hear, and who justify themselves as they carry out the 'execution'. Jesus himself stood in a long line of faithful prophets; the New Testament tells us also of the martyrdom of Stephen and refers to others; the pattern continues to the present day. The reports we have of many who maintain their witness to Christ even to death are awesome and humbling.

Threatened apostasy and judgment

So while Moses and Aaron fall on their faces (presumably in prayer, and probably in fear of both the congregation and the Lord), who will act first? Caleb and Joshua testify (vv. 5–9), making points of two kinds:

- Physical: the land is good and highly desirable; the inhabitants can be overcome.
- Spiritual: the Lord will bring them into the land—only do not rebel against him.

Of course, these statements are interwoven, since the Lord acts in the physical world. The argument is strong and cogent—and cuts no ice at all with the depressed and disillusioned congregation. Fortunately for the leaders (and, unfortunately for us, this does not happen often), the glory of the Lord appears to the Israelites and stops them in their tracks (v. 10). We are not told whether they stayed while Moses conversed with God. If they did, then they did not hear the words, for in 14:39 Moses has to pass the Lord's message on to them (compare John 12:28–30).

As in Exodus 32:7–14, the Lord offers to scrap the Israelites and start again with Moses' descendants. As before, Moses prays that God will not do that for the sake of his own reputation (vv. 13–16; compare Exodus 32:12) and because it would be against his own revealed character (vv. 17–19; compare Exodus 32:13, which bases the appeal on the promises made to Abraham and his descendants). The formula in verse 18 was given in slightly longer form in Exodus 34:6–7, when Moses asked the Lord to 'show him his glory'. This may be taken, therefore, as a sort of core creed. It outlines important positive characteristics of God, with some warning.

- He is merciful, gracious, slow to anger, forgiving, and abounding in steadfast love and faithfulness
- *But* he does not clear the guilty, visiting parents' iniquity on to their children

The 'sins of the fathers'

The idea of making children pay for their parents' sins is rightly offensive to most people today. The Old Testament itself comments on it in Jeremiah (31:29–30) and Ezekiel (18:2–32). Yet it is all too plain that, in our experience of life, children do suffer because of their parents' (and more remote ancestors') sins. This is how God has made the world. We do have the power to hurt others, directly and indirectly. As with painful childbirth, this situation is not 'God's will, so we must let it be'. We work together with God by the means put within us to change the situation, and God assures us that his will is not ever to 'punish the wrong person' for sin. Here we are led into the mystery of the atonement, that it *is* possible to bear someone else's suffering. The atonement made by Christ is related to the many ordinary actions in life where people voluntarily undergo suffering (or merely put themselves out) for others, or suffer because of others' needs or sins and forgive. The love that is demonstrated and engendered in such acts may help us in some way to understand why God arranged things so.

Verses 20–25 show us the well-known picture of residual suffering after sin is forgiven. The world is organized like this too. Why it is so is beyond my comprehension, but it does show very clearly the responsibility given to human beings, and the impossibility of just 'saying sorry and making it all OK again'. Mistakes are not wiped away but redeemed. And that is very difficult, for God as well as for us.

A PRAYER

Lord, forgive those who have hurt, wronged or offended me. Merciful Saviour, help me to mean what I've just said. I renounce all bitterness and resentment. Scrape them off me and put them out of reach. Help me to love others as you have loved me. Amen.

'Oops, sorry!' Is Not Enough

A certain woman gave her husband such a wonderful birthday present that he couldn't believe it was genuine and walked out. On learning his mistake, he returned to say, 'Sorry about that.' But the present was gone.

Analogies are rarely perfect, and there are major differences between the fairy story above and the account of the Israelites' response to God's offered gift. Nevertheless, it is closer to the situation than the popular account of 'the harsh Old Testament God who won't let people repent but wipes them out'. The people had rejected what God had done for them in liberating them from slavery, and in providing for them in the desert. They wished to stone the leaders who had brought them to this point, and to return to Egypt. This would have been an apostasy greater than the golden calf incident, and more blameworthy. Some judgment is called for, some demonstration of the seriousness of rebellion against the Lord that would serve as a warning for future generations—a salutary warning, a salvation-preserving warning.

Judgment and forgiveness

Christians faced with this idea, of course, must decide how it fits with their theology of God, sin and judgment. There are a number of common responses.

It may be said that the events in this passage, including the action and words of God, happened as stated and demonstrate God's permanent abhorrence of sin. Some, on the other hand, hold that the events are not to be thought of as historical but as a way of expressing the holiness of God. Yet others would say that the events didn't happen like this—or at least the Israelites interpreted the action wrongly as God's express judgment—and that the conception of God presented here is out of kilter with the New Testament.

One might think that these positions have nothing in common, but that would be a mistake, for probably all of them accept that God is a gracious God who takes the initiative in saving and blessing people. We should take discipleship very seriously indeed. The real differences concern:

- God's actual intervention in the world. Does he act directly in physical ways? Or is it all 'behind the scenes' so that 'you can't catch God actually doing anything'?

- The possibility that such severe judgment might be God's intention.

Not just an Old Testament problem

These are real difficulties and lead to deep divisions between believers. So is there any way of reaching a closer agreement or at least understanding of one another? First, it is worth noting the strict pronouncements of judgment in the New Testament, even or especially on the lips of Jesus, and the actual judgments described there (such as the fate of Ananias and Sapphira, Acts 5:1–11). We should also note the way that disasters happen in the world, the world over which, according to Christian thinking, God has full control.

This narrative represents a major turning point in the Israelites' fortunes. Up to this point they have been looking forward to making smooth progress towards conquering and settling in the land of Canaan, promised so long ago to their ancestor Abraham. Their refusal to believe God and obey leads to their own forfeiture of entry into this inheritance. However, God has not given up on them. Despite the fact that parents' sins affect ('are visited on') the children, God is determined to bless them and he perseveres.

The passage as a whole fits our experience of mistakes and wrongdoing which leave a painful legacy that God's forgiveness does not remove. They therefore speak to us of the difficulty of overcoming sin, of the need for more than 'well, never mind'. They point us, in fact, to the cross of Christ, where God himself pays the awful price of human sin.

FOR REFLECTION

'If only I hadn't…' Do you ever catch yourself saying this?
What would be a more fruitful redirection of your thinking?

RULES, INTENTION & *a* TEST CASE

The basic details of the regulation sections of this chapter may be set out quite briefly. So the *Idiot's Priestly Guide Book* might say (vv. 1–16):

Sacrifices are to be accompanied by the following:

	Cereal offering	Drink offering
Basic sacrifice:	0.1 ephah flour + 0.25 hin oil	0.25 hin wine
Ram	0.2 ephah flour + 0.33 hin oil	0.33 hin
Bull	0.3 ephah flour + 0.5 hin oil	0.5 hin

Probably most people will never need these instructions, but verse 14 is significant: it tells us that resident aliens who wished to offer a sacrifice might do so. This is a tacit acknowledgment that they were part of God's people and enjoyed God's favour (compare v. 29). We have glimpses of the fact that this happened fairly commonly in, for example, the story of Ruth, the references to Moses' wives, and the soldiers fighting for Israel, who came from other tribes, perhaps most famously Uriah the Hittite. The many prophetic diatribes against the surrounding nations have the concern that the people of Israel should not be led into idolatry and the practices of those nations, including 'sacred prostitution' and child sacrifice. Privilege carries responsibility, as we have seen (compare v. 15–16; Leviticus 24:16).

Worshippers should offer part of the first batch of bread of each new season to the Lord (vv. 17–21). The clear message is that God has priority. Our love for him is primary and should be shown in the way we live. At times, this provides a sort of Elijah's widow test: with only enough for one meal for her son and herself, would she give first to the prophet of the Lord? Yes, she would, and the Lord provided her with many meals in the days following (1 Kings 17). But this is not to be the motive, and few have experienced such miraculous provision. Nevertheless, many, many people testify to the fact that God has met their needs when they have put this principle into practice. It is confirmed by Jesus himself in Matthew 6:33.

Next comes a section on unintentional failures. For these, a congregation must bring a sin offering (male goat) and a burnt offering (young bull), plus cereal and drink offerings. An individual brings a sin offering (female goat, one year old) and, presumably, cereal and drink offerings.

Then comes a most important contrast, which might come to some readers as a complete surprise. Sins committed 'with a high hand' (v. 30) cannot be dealt with by sacrifice. The context gives us some clue to the meaning, for it represents an affront to the Lord and despising his word. Certain biblical data are difficult to fit together. David was guilty of adultery and virtual murder (almost a contract killing) in the case of Uriah (2 Samuel 11:2–5, 14–15) but he escaped the just penalty of the law (stoning for adultery, similarly for murder, though it would have been difficult to convict). Perhaps this gives us a hint of the fact that God's grace goes beyond what is reasonable and into the realm of the flabbergasting. But is it one rule for the rich and another for the poor? Christ's coming makes it abundantly clear that God deals with each person equally.

Remembering God at all times

The final verses of the chapter are an example of 'the practice of the presence of God'. The Israelites are to put fringes and blue cord at the corners of their garments to remind them to avoid following their own desires and to remember the Lord. Deuteronomy 6:6–9 commands that the Israelites should bind the commandments on their hands and forehead, signifying the need to remember God at all times. This passage has led to the practice among contemporary Jews of putting a little piece of scroll in a small box and binding it to the arm and/or forehead. This was not the original intention of the command—but it might still be a useful reminder. Similarly, sewing blue fringes on your clothes might be both a reminder and a conversation starter, but it is not necessary for salvation (compare Galatians 5:2).

The incident of the man gathering sticks on the sabbath being stoned to death (vv. 32–36) is similar to other strict judgments that we have come across. I once heard someone on the radio read it in a scornful voice as if it was pathetic and there was nothing else to say. See the comment on Leviticus 10 (pp. 56–57); 24 (pp. 96–97); and Numbers 14 (pp. 138–139) for similar situations—and note that this man's family was not put to death.

FOR CONSIDERATION
Is there a suitable 'badge' or sign or symbol that I could wear without embarrassment and that would be of some help in my Christian life and witness?

KORAH, DATHAN & ABIRAM REBEL

This chapter tells of more rebellion concerning leadership, presumably motivated by pride and resentment. Aaron comes under attack in chapters 16 and 17 as the question is raised of whether the people need such a person in such a role. Four rebels are mentioned in verse 1: Korah (on his own also in vv. 6, 16, 32, 49) of the tribe of Levi, and Dathan, Abiram and On of the tribe of Reuben. So Korah alone is a Levite, with authority to officiate in public worship, and it is he who is instructed, 'with all his company' (250 of them, according to verse 35), to prepare censers with incense on them. The others seem to constitute a separate group of rebels, but they are united in their grumbling about the leaders. On gets no further mention, and it may be that his name is due to a mistake by a scribe, who should have copied 'Eliab, son of Pallu' (as in 26:8–9).

Moses, and Dathan and Abiram

Dathan and Abiram are mentioned on their own in verses 12–14. Moses sends for them but they refuse to come, and Moses prays against them (somewhat petulantly?) (v. 15). It is not unusual to find such prayers—imprecations—in the Old Testament on the lips of reputable people, for example, Jeremiah (12:1–3; 17:18; 18:19–23; 20:12), and there are many in the Psalms (for example, 109:6–20). Strictly speaking, they are asking for justice, not personal vengeance, but the New Testament requires us to go further—to pray *for* our enemies. Jesus gave us the pattern of prayer, 'Father, forgive them' (Luke 23:34), and Stephen followed in his footsteps with 'Lord, do not hold this sin against them' (Acts 7:60). Few of us can blame Moses or the others for their outbursts, especially since very few have suffered on behalf of the people as much as they did, but they are still not our ideal role model.

Moses and Korah

The thrust of the complaint seems to be (again) that the leaders have a privileged position that ought to be the right of a larger body. This time the complaint is allegedly on behalf of the whole congregation (v. 3): they are all holy and the Lord is among them. This time it is directed against Moses *and* Aaron. Moses defends his brother Aaron and accuses Korah and the other Levites of not being satisfied with the great privilege of being Levites, and of seeking the priesthood as well. He suggests a test in a very daring way and proclaims that 'the man the Lord chooses shall be the holy one' (v. 7). The test is different from that of Elijah's sacrifice test with the prophets of Baal (1 Kings 18) in that the censers are already lit—they do not ask God to light them. It is not clear what sort of demonstration Moses expected, but the judgment in Leviticus 10 on Nadab and Abihu, who brought 'strange fire before the Lord', at least alerts the reader to the possibility of fire from heaven. It would seem that incense offering was dangerous in Old Testament times! Good King Uzziah became a leper by usurping the priests' prerogative and offering incense (2 Chronicles 27:16–21).

Presumably we are not to think of the men with censers as going down 'alive into Sheol', that is, the place of the dead (v. 33). It has been suggested that the cause of this sudden descent was that they were on a *kewir*, a muddy bog that can develop a hard crust over it but may split open. The text does not give any hint about this—though it may be possible—but stresses the divine nature of the act.

As with the golden calf incident, people are given the chance to separate themselves from Korah, Dathan and Abiram (vv. 23–27) and their rebellion before the double judgment is carried out. First the ground opens up and swallows up Korah (we must presume Dathan and Abiram also, though they are not mentioned in v. 32). Then fire comes down to consume the men offering incense (v. 35).

It is noteworthy that Moses does not say in verse 30 that if the ground swallows the men up, then he will be vindicated. Rather, it will be seen that 'these men have despised the Lord'. It is nothing simply to oppose a human being, but to oppose the Lord's appointment of a human being is deadly serious (compare also v. 11). Of course, there is a trap here for those who *assume* that they have the 'divine right of Christian leaders'. Jesus gives advice as to how the danger might be minimized: 'Whoever wishes to be first among you must be slave of all' (Mark 10:44; compare John 13:12–15).

FOR REFLECTION

'The slave of all'—including the people we take for granted and those who habitually annoy us? How long can you keep it up?

A PERMANENT REMINDER

The fire that consumed the men offering incense is deemed to have purified and consecrated the censers used (v. 38). Perhaps there is an indication that those who died have not been totally rejected, for they seem to have been regarded as an acceptable sacrifice in some sense. Their deaths have purified the bronze censers. Whether this is so or not, the bronze censers are hammered out to make a covering for the altar (v. 39). The verb signifies 'overlaying' or 'plating'. Exodus 38:2 says that Bezalel 'overlaid the altar of burnt offering with bronze' and the Septuagint says that he used these particular censers. We don't know, therefore, whether a replacement covering is intended: an altar made of wood (even acacia wood) would not function well without a substantial metal covering. The theological point is emphatic: incense signifies an approach to God and this must be strictly on *his* terms. The lesson about God's holiness is once more reinforced. A constant reminder is instituted. The situation seems to be improving, but the very next day...

A bad reaction—and further judgment

'But they cursed the name of God, who had authority over these plagues, and they did not repent and give him glory'. These words from Revelation 16:9 (compare vv. 11, 21) are reminiscent of the Israelites' reaction to the judgments dealt with earlier in the chapter. They are expressed in more homely fashion by Charlie Brown and Lucy. 'All you have to do is say sorry and ask nicely'—[pause to consider the suggestion]—'I'd rather die.' Instead of examining their actions, learning from them and changing their attitude, the people's self-righteous anger takes over. This frightening feature of human beings is what makes Christian discipleship so hard and sometimes dangerous. Cain is so blinded by resentment when Abel's offering is accepted and his is rejected that he refuses God's gracious offer to 'do well and be accepted' (Genesis 4:5–7).

God acts decisively once more, sending a plague, and threatens again to wipe them all out. This time it is Aaron, encouraged by Moses, who takes action. He stands between those who have already died from the plague and those who are about to die, and 'makes atonement' for them (vv. 46–47). This is not a regular method of making atonement and we do not know whether this action was regarded as a precedent for other situations. It clearly validates Aaron's high priesthood and that of all future high priests descended from Aaron. Incense was a symbol of prayer ascending to God, and God's answer in this situation is clear—prayer rejected. It is difficult to conceive of God as habitually deciding to destroy people and having to be dissuaded by (imperfect) human beings. Perhaps it is more in line with the rest of biblical teaching to interpret this as signifying that special intervention is needed to prevent their destruction. Why does God tell Moses and Aaron if he does not want them to intercede for the people?

Unfortunately for us (or fortunately, actually), God does not always intervene in this way, and the words of Shadrach, Meshach and Abednego continue to have poignant significance: 'If it be so [that is, if we are thrown into the furnace] our God whom we serve is able to deliver us… let him deliver us. But if not… [we will remain faithful to him]' (Daniel 3:17–18). Many believers have remained faithful though literally burnt to death. Many have experienced lesser deliverances (perhaps only from a youth club rumpus), and many have suffered non-deliverances. At such times, it is especially important to know that God remains in control.

FOR PRAYER AND MEDITATION

Lighten our darkness, we beseech thee, O Lord; and by thy great mercy defend us from all perils and dangers of this night; for the love of thy only Son, our Saviour, Jesus Christ. Amen.

Book of Common Prayer, Collect from Evening Prayer

This is a realistic and necessary prayer for many Christians throughout the world. Remember those who are in great peril today.

The STAFF *that* BUDDED

Aaron's divine authority accepted

We have been dealing with the establishment of the priesthood of
Aaron and his descendants, and the incident of the budding staff
decisively concludes the matter. This is expressly stated to be the
motive for putting twelve staffs in the tent of meeting 'before the
covenant' (that is, the ark of the covenant). Aaron's rod will produce
shoots, putting an end to the complaints that the Israelites make continually (v. 5). The text makes it clear that this is a miraculous intervention by the Lord, in that the very next day the rod has produced
buds, blossoms and ripe almonds.

It is possible that the almond was chosen because of its white
blossom, signifying purity. In one of Jeremiah's visions, he sees a rod
of almond (*shaqed*) which yields its message by means of a pun: 'I am
watching (*shoqed*) over my word to perform it' (Jeremiah 1:11–12).
Although no explanation is given, it is likely that Jeremiah's vision
alludes to this narrative in Numbers.

Aaron's staff is kept as yet another sign to remind the Israelites
of their origins and history, their dependence upon the Lord, the
divinely given institutions for public worship—and the dangers of
pride and presumption. Many churches have discovered afresh the
power of symbols and other types of non-verbal communication—
paintings, sculpture, banners, stained glass, music, dancing. The
Bible suggests that these *should* be used, but used alongside verbal
explanations. So, when the children ask about the twelve stones by
the side of the Jordan, the parents are to explain their meaning
(Joshua 4:20–24). The stones are an invitation and a stimulus to
questioning and further understanding. Even so, some symbolic
communication takes place at a level that goes beyond words. This is
what makes the Eucharist or service of Holy Communion so powerful for many.

An unbalanced response

The Israelites finally seem to realize that God is real and dangerous
(vv. 12–13) and that Aaron is God's chosen priest. Yet it is not a well-

balanced or reasonable view. They have not incorporated into it the abundant evidence of God's gracious initiative in choosing them to be his people and in delivering them from the land of Egypt. Samson's mother might have given them sound advice: 'If the Lord had meant to kill us, he would not have… shown us all these things' (Judges 13:22–23)! Peter's response in Luke 5 is more surprising. After a huge catch of fish he says, 'Go away from me, Lord, for I am a sinful man.' The same feeling of awe and unworthiness was experienced by Isaiah when he saw God in a vision in the temple (Isaiah 6). Many people in the Bible and throughout history up to the present time have felt diffident about accepting a call to serve God, recognizing both the great privilege and the great responsibility conveyed.

Today, it is just as difficult to 'get it right'. Probably, we are more obviously short on reverence and *therefore* short on appreciation. To be someone for whom Christ died, and therefore to be the personal concern of the creator of the entire universe, is quite beyond comprehension and yet we are generally less excited about it than those who simply receive a birthday card from the Queen. Even in churches that emphasize the mystic and awesome aspects of God, it is doubtful whether there is a keen enough appreciation of the fact that without God's grace we would all perish.

An incident from Elisha's life is illuminating. When surrounded by a huge enemy army, Elisha told his attendant that 'there are more with us than there are with them' and prayed that the Lord would *open his eyes*—not to give him a vision of something that wasn't there but to show him the reality of what was there (2 Kings 6:16–17). We know that many things are invisible but highly effective—viruses, germs and bacteria, gas, radiation. It is more difficult to take on board the fact that the spiritual realm is at least as real as any of these.

FOR REFLECTION

'Awe without joy is worse than joy without awe.' I wonder if it is.
But why should it be necessary to choose?

PROVISION *for* PRIESTS & LEVITES

'The labourer deserves to be paid.' So said Jesus as he sent out the seventy (or seventy-two) disciples to preach the gospel (Luke 10:7), and Paul elaborates on this principle in 1 Corinthians 9:4–14, mentioning specifically the fact that 'those who are employed in the temple service get their food from the temple, and those who serve at the altar share in what is sacrificed on the altar'. He thereby indicates his approval of the system that can be traced back to the earliest days of Israel's history.

Privileges and duties

There's no such thing as a free sacrificial lunch. Aaron and his descendants are to perform the priestly tasks and *to see that no one else does it*. Verse 1 literally says 'bear iniquity', which means 'bear responsibility' but is more pointed. They have the strict charge that 'any outsider who approaches [to arrogate to himself the priest's role] is to be put to death' (v. 7). The Levites are 'given' to the priests as their assistants. They have a privileged role also but are not to approach the utensils (or vessels) of the sanctuary or the altar. The priests are to see to it that everything is done in accordance with God's instructions, so that the whole nation may be blessed (1 Samuel 2:12ff). This may seem like a tall order, but the bad example of priests leads to corruption throughout the people of Israel, and a good example has an influence that extends far and wide (see 1 Samuel 12:1–5, 19–25). Jesus himself expected *all* his followers to be salt and light—and the right sort of leaven (Matthew 5:13–16; 13:33; 16:6; compare 1 Corinthians 5:6–9).

The list of dues (vv. 9–19) includes various sacrifices (the parts not wholly burnt or given back to the worshipper), the gifts made to the Lord, the first fruits of the land (note that only those who are ritually clean may eat of these gifts, possibly a cause of friction for teenagers in priestly families? 'My friends don't have that sort of restriction'), and the devoted things. This last one might come as a surprise because the 'devoted things', or those things which were 'put to the ban' or wholly devoted to the Lord, were normally either completely destroyed or restricted for holy purposes—silver and gold could not be destroyed. Leviticus 27:21 has already mentioned fields released in the jubilee that are 'devoted' and become 'the priest's holding'.

The phrase 'covenant of salt for ever' (v. 19) is obscure. All offerings had to have some salt with them (Leviticus 2:13), as did incense (Exodus 30:35: 'blended with salt, pure and holy') and there is a reference to the kingship given to David and his descendants 'for ever... by a covenant of salt' (2 Chronicles 13:5). The most likely explanation is that salt as a preservative signifies permanence. The covenant will not go rotten on them—ever.

The Lord is your portion

Priests had no land allotment because the Lord was their 'share and possession'. The symbolism is that of people entirely focused upon serving God and finding their security in God. I was once asked by a visitor to the Maramon Convention (a huge annual Christian gathering in India) if I was paid a salary, and why I didn't live by faith. I replied that I didn't think I would do too well. I would probably live 'by hinting' (that is, to friends that we were looking for the Lord to supply our needs). The principle of supporting one's religious ministers has always been accepted by most groups, but we don't always get the balance right. At times, ministers are poor to the point of wondering where the next meal is to come from, and in other situations the religious establishment has achieved control of wealth and lived at a standard far beyond that of those they 'serve'—and in a manner at odds with what Jesus expected.

The Levites are addressed in verses 25–32. They are to give a tithe (a tenth, see Leviticus 27) of a tithe to the priests and it was to be the best part. The rest of the Israelite tithes is theirs to eat—only they must not profane the holy gifts, presumably by eating in an unclean state, or perhaps by treating them irreverently in some way.

There is no specific requirement that tithes should go to support the poor or other worthy causes. All Israelites had this duty, as we have seen (for example, Leviticus 19:10; 23:22).

FOR REFLECTION AND PRAYER

Leaders are called to be humble servants but not beggars. Are your own leaders given the right sort of support?

The RED HEIFER

Provision for those who touch death

For the benefit of townies, a heifer is a cow that has borne only one calf, if any . The Hebrew simply says 'cow' but the animal is not to have 'had the yoke laid on it' (v. 2), that is, it has not been employed in agricultural work and so is presumed to be young. The animal is to be without blemish, as is usual for sacrifices, but elsewhere bulls are specified for sacrifice and only here is the colour of the animal important. It is assumed that the red signifies blood. Another unique feature is that the blood is listed in the elaboration of what is to be burnt (v. 5)—all except for a sprinkling of blood for the tent of meeting (v. 4). Elsewhere the blood is taken from the animal before it is burnt, even from the whole burnt offering (Leviticus 1:3–5). Furthermore, the ashes of the heifer were kept for future use, whereas other sacrifices were to be consumed or disposed of within three days. It is not clear how often a red heifer would have to be burnt—the ashes could not have lasted all that long.

Attempts are being made today by ultra-orthodox Jews to produce a cow that is perfectly red, with no spots or patches of a different colour, so that this ritual can be carried out and they will be ready to reinstitute the system of sacrifices when the temple is rebuilt. Some would like to demolish the Dome of the Rock in Jerusalem and build the temple there. It is evident from our reading of Leviticus and Numbers that Christians should not be able to support this venture, since we believe that Christ made the old Levitical sacrifices redundant. It is also clear that this is the wrong sort of focus on the term 'without blemish'. Blood was never perfectly drained from sacrificial victims: the requirement was symbolic. And surely it is unlikely that the ancient Israelites ever subjected their reddish heifers to the sort of examination being applied today—nor would they ever have thought of such a thing.

The sacrifice involves at least two priests—Eleazar and another.

- The heifer is taken outside the camp and slaughtered (in the presence of Eleazar, not Aaron) (v. 3).
- Eleazar sprinkles blood seven times towards the front of the tent of meeting (so he has come back into the camp) (v. 4).
- The heifer is burnt (in the presence of Eleazar) completely (v. 5).

- 'The priest' throws cedarwood, hyssop and crimson material on to the fire along with the heifer (v. 6).
- 'The priest' washes his clothes and himself and is unclean until the evening (v. 7).
- 'The one who burns the heifer' (a third priest) washes similarly (v. 8).
- A clean person deposits the ashes in a clean place outside the camp for future use in the 'water of cleansing'. He washes his clothes and is unclean until the evening (vv. 9–10).

The narrative moves on to talk about contact with corpses. It seems to breathe an anxious spirit that is quite understandable. Dead bodies decay and stink; they breed maggots and are easily associated with contagion. The ancients had experience of death by disease and an unexplained death was a source of worry. Hence the strict rules for dealing with unwitting contact with death: it would make good sense hygienically and psychologically to have prescribed procedures, a defence against hypochondria.

The general rule (vv. 10b–13) is that those who touch a dead body are unclean for seven days. They must wash on the third and seventh day (with the water for cleansing, v. 13); otherwise they remain unclean and are to be cut off from Israel. In the case of a death in a tent, precautions were taken against airborne disease in a confined space (all who enter or are already in the tent, as well as open vessels, are unclean) and everything at risk was to be sprinkled with a mixture of red heifer ashes and running water.

The final verses are odd but not untypical. The water for cleansing makes the unclean sprinkled one clean and the clean sprinkler unclean (though only until the evening). There is thus a symbol of one who, in cleansing, becomes unclean, as the heifer without blemish takes away the blemishes of the sinful.

FOR MEDITATION

The symbolism of the red heifer 'cries out for fulfilment…
The inadequacy is not only that of the victim… but of the tediously
slow cleansing and the wholly external realm in which it operated.
The conscience, as Hebrews 9:9, 13–14 points out, was untouched'
(Derek Kidner, Leviticus—Deuteronomy, p. 47)

In what ways are Christians better off?

MOSES' WORST CHAPTER YET

Moses loses his sister (v. 1), his brother (v. 29) and his inheritance (v. 12) in the space of this chapter. First of all, we have a brief note of Miriam's death at Kadesh in the wilderness of Zin, without obituary. This seems rather sad in view of the prominent part she played in leading the celebrations when Israel came out of Egypt (Exodus 15). And at the end we have a note of Aaron's death on Mount Hor after passing on the vestments of office to his son Eleazar (whom we have already met in the red heifer ritual). Aaron's death is similar to that of Moses. Both die on top of a mountain; both are under the same judgment: they will not enter the promised land themselves.

There are two places called 'Meribah' (meaning 'contention' or 'quarrel') mentioned in the Pentateuch: here in verse 13, and in Exodus 17:7, where we also find the name 'Massah' (meaning 'proof' or 'test'). Aaron's judgment is puzzling because there is no hint that Aaron was on the side of the rebels at 'Massah and Meribah' in Exodus 17; and there is no mention of Aaron's having done anything wrong at 'Meribah' in Numbers 20.

Perhaps Aaron is included with 'the people' in Exodus 17. Unfortunately, we know that he was capable of slipping up in his discernment and loyalty. If it is supposed that Aaron is judged for the incident at Meribah in Numbers 20, then we can only assume that it is because he was associated with Moses' action. The reason given for Aaron's exclusion from entry to the promised land (v. 24) is not necessarily the full and complete reason. In the narrative about the conquest of Canaan, three reasons are given for Israel's failure to defeat and occupy the whole land immediately: disobedience (see Judges 2:1–4); to stop wild animals from becoming too numerous in empty land (Deuteronomy 7:22); and to give training in war (Judges 3:1–2). So perhaps God also had in mind the fact that new situations benefit from new and fresh leaders?

Water from the rock again, but...

The people again grumble and complain against Moses because they have no water. 'Things were better than this in Egypt': again their selective memories paint them a rosy picture of the time when they were actually enslaved in Egypt. If a people want to achieve political and economic liberation, their situation will usually get worse before it gets better. Those who begin to work, for instance, with bonded labourers in India find that, the moment the labourers begin to believe in and stand up for their rights, thugs are brought in to beat them into deeper submission. Reformers who work against the excessive interest rate charges there (12 per cent *per month*, compound interest; that is, 390 per cent APR) have to reckon with the fact that a person on the point of starvation will do anything in order to survive a little longer. No doubt the Israelites had a hard lesson to learn, and we who are used to a comparatively easy life will probably sympathize with them more than the text does.

The nature of Moses' sin is not clear but it has been extensively discussed. The clues given in the Old Testament are in verse 8 ('command the rock') contrasted with verse 11 ('Moses struck the rock twice'), and verse 12 ('because you did not believe [or trust] in me, to show my holiness before the eyes of the Israelites'). Moses' strong words in verse 10 can easily be taken as a failure to assign credit to the Lord for the miracle (compare Deuteronomy 32:50–51).

Edom earns permanent resentment

The Israelites need to pass through the territory of Edom, and they make the reasonable request that they will pay for any water that they consume *en route* (v. 19). The Edomites, descended from Esau, Jacob's brother, and regarded as kinsmen of the Israelites in some texts, refuse and bring out an army to show that they mean it. Israel often looked back to this event with great bitterness—and it was reinforced by later treachery (Obadiah 11–14). Understandable… and yet… How is the cycle of international killing to be halted and reversed unless 'reasonable grounds for hatred' are overcome?

FOR REFLECTION

'They angered the Lord at the waters of Meribah, and it went ill with Moses on their account; for they made his spirit bitter, and he spoke words that were rash' (Psalm 106:32–33).

Are you adequately protected against those who drive us to distraction today?

COMPLETE DESTRUCTION

Three battles are described here, at least the first and the last involving the complete destruction of the people opposing Israel (see comment on Leviticus 27, pp. 106–107; also Joshua 6:17, 21; 1 Samuel 15:3, 9–11, 20–23).

Answered prayer or coincidence?

We should expect the God and Father of our Lord Jesus Christ not to be impressed by the offer of the Israelites: 'Give these people into our hands and we will destroy their towns completely' (v. 2). Perhaps all we can do in the face of such horror is to remind ourselves of some basic facts.

- The thinking of the Pentateuch concerning the destruction of the Canaanites is that God gave them 400 years to repent and they refused. The judgment comes as a last resort.

- The practice of 'putting to the ban' or 'devoting to destruction' was a well-known practice of the time. It was built into the Israelites' thinking, but their understanding of the need for it was connected with purification, unlike that of the Canaanites themselves.

- God apparently chooses not to force his people into making quick progress in understanding (even today).

- If God had not shown amazing forbearance with these brutal people, we, who are the spiritual descendants of the Israelites, would not be here as believers today.

- It is possible that God answers our prayers for reasons different from those that we imagine. When it comes to understanding God's purposes, we are all simpletons.

Violence, and resistance, today

There is no warrant from this chapter or any other in the Old Testament for Christians to assume that ethnic cleansing in any form is acceptable to God. Disasters continue in the world and no doubt many are *in some way* related to judgment, but the Christian's mandate is clear from Matthew 28:19: 'Go therefore and make disciples [not corpses] of all nations, baptizing them…'. God does not need and does not ask for help in judging his creation. It is generally agreed today that the medieval Crusades were badly motivated and badly carried out, at times in a most unholy way. But there are serious challenges today when force is used against Christians or those perceived to be Christians. The following situations are well documented:

- Christians living under Shari'ah law in *some* Muslim countries may be executed for sharing their faith, especially in such a way as to lead to the conversion of a Muslim. Is 'outside political intervention' called for in any of these situations?

- In some countries, systematic annihilation of Christians is being attempted. In others there is ethnic violence on other grounds. What can the international community do that might be constructive?

- Terrorism has been perpetrated, assisted and harboured by individuals, organizations and nations. What political and other action ought to be attempted?

The battles mentioned in the latter part of this chapter were celebrated in song and incorporated into the 'official hymn book' of Israel, the Psalms. Ex-choirboys and choirgirls will probably find that 'Sihon, king of the Amorites, and Og the king of Bashan' still trips off the tongue very readily from Psalms 135:11 and 136:19. Jephthah included the victory against Sihon when he outlined the past deeds of the Lord on Israel's behalf to the aggressive Ammonites (Judges 11:19–23) and challenged them with the thought that they were taking the place of the defeated Amorites.

FOR REFLECTION AND PRAYER

Lord, despite our past and continuing sinfulness, you have delivered us in time of war. Grant us and our leaders wisdom and the will to do what is right in your eyes. Bring peace to the holy land, where people struggle with and kill each other, all imagining that they serve the one true God.

LOOK *at the* SNAKE & LIVE

John's Gospel draws our attention to the important narrative of the 'burning fiery serpents' when Jesus says, 'As Moses lifted up the serpent in the wilderness, so must the Son of Man be lifted up, that whoever believes in him may have eternal life' (John 3:14–15). This is, of course, immediately followed by the best-known verse in John's Gospel, 3:16, 'the gospel in a nutshell': 'God so loved the world that he gave his only Son, so that everyone who believes in him may not perish but may have eternal life.' John, therefore, makes an explicit connection between the bronze snake on the pole in the desert and Christ on the cross— between salvation from snakebite and salvation from sin.

The same message, then and now

When studying such connections, it is usually profitable to ask whether the original Old Testament passage had the same essential meaning and how the New Testament makes use of it. Here in Numbers, the desert had again become a place of grumbling and rebellion against God. And, as before, God sent a judgment upon the Israelites, to chasten them and persuade them to turn back to him.

T.E. Lawrence has given graphic accounts of the dangers of snakes in this region:

> *The plague of snakes which had been with us since our first entry into Sirhan,*
> *rose today to a memorable height, and became a terror... this year the valley*
> *seemed creeping with horned vipers and puff-adders, cobras and black snakes.*
> *By night movement was dangerous: and at last we found it necessary to walk*
> *with sticks, beating the bushes while we stepped warily through on bare feet...*
> *they got so on our nerves that even the boldest of us feared to touch the*
> *ground. (*Revolt in the Desert, *pp. 131–2; quoted in Raymond Brown,*
> The Message of Numbers, *pp. 185–6)*

The judgment came through something that was already there in the desert, so what might have happened if the Israelites had been obedient? At least three types of divine solution seem to be well known in Christian experience: God may remove the source of the problem; or he may keep us safe through it (that is, not let us be bitten); or he may continue to bring healing as we continue to get bitten. The third solution clearly corresponds to the Israelites' situation: they might get bitten, but they *need not* die. All that was required was to look at the bronze snake that Moses had set up on the pole. Clearly the analogy with faith is very close: as the old hymn puts it, 'there's a light for a look at the Saviour... turn your eyes upon Jesus'.

Why a snake?

Many have wondered about the choice of object for the top of the pole, and all sorts of ingenious answers have been given. Nachmanides, a Spanish rabbi born in 1194, said, 'Because the sight of a serpent is harmful to persons who had been bitten they were given the cure of looking at an artificial serpent, to make them realize that it is God who preserves and keeps alive.' One scholar thought that it was a deliberate use of Egyptian power symbols (both the pole and the snake), though the logic of this is hard to follow. In Egypt, model snakes were worn to ward off snakebites but this would seem to be a reason for *not* using a bronze snake. Calvin believed that a 'mode of preservation was chosen... discordant with human reason' so that the people would realize that healing was through God's power alone. Perhaps the reddish colour of the snake (as with the red heifer) reminded the Israelites of the blood of sacrifice (G. Wenham). Whatever the merits of these suggestions, there are some clear resonances in other parts of the Old Testament, the most obvious being the narrative in Genesis 3 where Eve and Adam are led into temptation and sin by the snake. Thus the physical healing that came from looking at the serpent on the pole also speaks directly of the fact that God accepts our repentance and faith, and forgives.

The difference, of course, is that the serpent was only bronze and only a symbol of sin and distress. Jesus was both a real human being and the true Son of God, mysteriously bearing our sin 'in his body on the cross' (1 Peter 2:24).

FOR MEDITATION

Amazing love! O what sacrifice!
The Son of God, given for me.
My debt he pays, and my death he dies,
That I might live.

Graham Kendrick

SORRY I CAN'T HELP YOU (WINK)

This is an interesting story, but also very puzzling in that Balaam says all the right things and seems to be consistent, whereas the Lord seems to change his mind and act unreasonably. After all, Balaam refuses to go with the visitors and insists that he can't go against what God will give him to say. Perhaps it was like this:

Scene 1 (verses 5–14)

Balak's men: Come and curse Israel for me.
Balaam: *[Thinks: This could be profitable but it's tricky.]* I'll enquire of the Lord. *[Thinks: But I'm afraid I know what he'll say.]* *[To the Lord.]* There are some men who want me to curse Israel. What do you think?
God: Absolutely not. I have blessed them.
Balaam: *[To the men.]* Sorry, boys. I wish there was a way to help you but the Lord won't let me.

Scene 2 (verses 15–21)

Balak's men: Come and curse Israel. It'll be well worth your while.
Balaam: It's not the money. I just can't do it. But don't go away. I'll see if there is anything helpful the Lord might tell me. *[Winks.]*
God: OK. Go with the men. But only do what I tell you.
Balaam: Right, Lord. *[Thinks: Maybe there will be some profit in this after all.]*

Scene 3 (verses 22–35)

Balaam's donkey speaks—we are not told about the mechanism. But an angel explains the situation to Balaam. 'Angel' means 'messenger' (of God) and they occur in both Old and New Testaments.

Angel: If your donkey hadn't turned aside just now, I would have killed you. Your way is perverse before me.
Balaam: *[Trembling, having temporarily forgotten about making a profit.]* OK. Sorry, I'll go home.

Angel:	No, now you're here, carry on. But speak only what I tell you to speak.
Balaam:	Right. Yes, of course. [Thinks: Drat.]

The suggestion that Balaam wanted to find a way of going along with Balak finds support in Deuteronomy 23:4–5 and Joshua 24:9–10: 'the Lord refused to listen to him'—that is, presumably, his unspoken thoughts. I wonder if you have ever been tempted to try to fool God in some way? Of course it's ridiculous, but it does happen: for example, perhaps you don't let on that you hate the idea of a particular job, in case he calls you to do it?

So Balaam goes with the men and meets up with Balak, who 'sacrificed oxen and sheep and sent them to Balaam' (v. 40). This would be a sort of feast for an honoured guest. How honoured or how uneasy Balaam felt, we are not told. Many people of conviction have struggled with the question of what constitutes support for wrongdoing or corruption, and Abraham's policy of not taking payment from certain sources seems to be a wise one (Genesis 14:22–24). If Balaam had had any discernment at all, he would have realized that to refuse to do Balak's bidding was dangerous—and to disobey the Lord deliberately was more dangerous still. Christians often face situations where compromise seems the most attractive course of action —or even the only possibility. Certainly there are no easy or universal answers. The best way forward would seem to be to talk to and pray with others facing the same issues.

A business out in the East required its drivers to comply with dishonest procedures or be sacked. Christians who worked there felt that they could not afford to refuse and so deprive their family of any income. They got together and prayed and in the course of the next year managed to get the firm to change its policy. We don't always hear of such happy endings but we know that God is not defeated by any difficulties.

FOR PRAYER

Pray for those who are in situations where they feel they should speak out but hesitate because of fear or simply the desire to avoid being unpleasant. Pray for those who speak out because they don't care about being unpleasant. Pray that God may help you always to act in the way that pleases him.

HOPES *of* CURSING THWARTED TWICE

Impressive but useless

Seven altars and seven double sacrifices (bull plus ram) probably impressed Balak but it didn't impress God. There is perhaps a hint that Balaam didn't rate them too highly either ('Stay here beside *your* offerings', v. 3), although he was the one who called for the elaborate ritual. Perhaps it was necessary to give Balak the impression that Balaam was an important man—so that he wouldn't execute Balaam later when he found the 'services rendered' unsatisfactory.

That is not to say, however, that impressive liturgy is worthless. Much of what we do in worship is for *our* benefit, so that we may more easily recognize what we do not see—the reality and immeasurable greatness of God. Hymns and psalms, light, symbols, pictures, poetry and well-fashioned language *can* all play a part in reminding us of the truth that we profess, and so nurture our faith. Many later passages in the Old Testament (as well as in the New) also remind us that there is a spiritual dimension to all this. The Spirit himself is active in igniting our hearts, and therefore we should not grieve him by 'solemn assemblies with iniquity' (Isaiah 1:13). Balaam knew that he was going along with a badly motivated plan and that these sacrifices would be of no use to Balak. He had told Balak this in words, but he had managed to communicate something else, perhaps by the way he said things (maybe 'he seemed to them to be jesting', like Lot in Genesis 19:14) or by his actions, which seemed to contradict his words.

The word from God is unequivocal when Balaam returns from his aside with God: 'How can I curse whom God has not cursed? How can I denounce those whom the Lord has not denounced?' (v. 8). There is also an allusion to the covenant with Abraham in 'Who can count the dust of Jacob' (numerous descendants) and 'Let me die the death of the upright, and let my end be like his!' (that is, 'blessing oneself by Jacob' as foretold in Genesis 22:18; 26:4—though the NRSV interprets this differently). Admittedly, we should not expect Balak to be a student of Israelite covenant theology, but the message is clear enough.

Persevering against God

So why should Balak persevere? Why not realize you can't beat 'em and try to join 'em? Amazingly he has two more attempts to get the result he requires. The main reason is probably the difference between magic and faith in Yahweh. Magic is a way of manipulating God or the gods or supernatural forces in order to get what *you* want. Faith in Yahweh requires finding out what he wants and obeying. It is worrying that the Lord sometimes lets us think that we have succeeded in imposing our will on him and frustrating his own purposes. For it *is* possible for a while to stop good work from proceeding. It *is* possible to exploit others and take what is rightly theirs. It *is* possible to put stumbling blocks in the way of others and cause them to fall—and in the long term it is one of the most dangerous things to do, especially with regard to children (Matthew 18:6–7). This course of action seems to be the secret that Balaam hit upon, as we shall see.

In verse 25, Balak seems to be getting the message: better to refrain from saying anything than to give a blessing where a curse has been requested. But he still persists in his plan and asks for one last attempt to be made (vv. 27–30). We shall find out the results of this in the next reading.

Achior, leader of the Ammonites, got it right in the (Apocryphal) book of Judith (5:20–21) at a much later period of history: 'If there is any oversight in this people and they sin against their God and we find out their offence, then we can go up and defeat them. But if they are not a guilty nation, then let my lord pass by them, for their Lord and God will defend them, and we shall become the laughingstock of the whole world.'

A PRAYER

O God, my Saviour and my Lord, when I try to make you in my image, stop me. Dispel from me the illusion that I can manipulate you and get away with it in the long term. Let the mind of Christ inform and form me. Make me a true disciple and follower of Jesus Christ your Son, for his name's sake, Amen.

69 NUMBERS 24

A FULL & FINAL BACKFIRE BLESSING

In his third location, Balaam sees Israel camping tribe by tribe, the Spirit comes upon him and he utters his third oracle, the most comprehensive yet. There is some important, though tantalizing, information here about the phenomenon of prophecy. We gather from verse 1 that Balaam's normal practice was to use 'omens', and it is not clear whether or to what extent this was acceptable practice.

Divining—and something better?

Some form of divination is condemned in 2 Kings 21:6, but other forms were used, such as examining the liver of an animal (hepatoscopy), or gazing into the eyes of a dying bird. Joshua 13:22 tells us that the Israelites killed 'Balaam the soothsayer' or 'the one who practised divination'. It would appear that later generations looked back on Balaam and judged him more harshly than the narrative in Numbers does. Paul's speech at Athens in the Areopagus may again be relevant: 'God has overlooked the times of human ignorance' (Acts 17:30).

A friend of mine, who had the gift of water-divining and used it for others' benefit in India, eventually came to the conclusion that it was a gift that God required her to give up for various reasons. This decision came about as the result of a remarkable experience of an answer to prayer for water. On the other hand, many use this gift apparently without harmful effects. A Hindu water diviner in Tumkur in India was invaluable in enabling a Christian vocational training centre to find an adequate water source on their land. He gave this service entirely free of charge.

Whatever answers we come to in this area, the text implies that there is a better way than divining techniques, as we have already seen in the description of Moses compared with other lesser prophets: he speaks with God face to face. In the two oracles set out in this chapter, Balaam is described as one whose eye is *open* (an uncertain word, but confirmed by 'uncovered' in v. 4). In other words, despite falling down (on his face), his eyes are open to see a vision of God. So Balaam claims something a little out of the ordinary here (in these two oracles only).

Long-term prophecies?

Many have taken the blessing in verse 9 as an encouragement to support Israel today. Yet this should not be taken as requiring sup-port at all costs and a muzzling of criticism. There is plenty of evidence in the Old Testament to suggest that God chastens and corrects his erring people, and that it is very difficult to predict when the right time is for Israelite expansion. What cannot be denied is that God demands right-eousness of individuals and of nations, especially the people to whom he has revealed his will.

Balaam goes on to add an unexpected prophecy at no extra charge (vv. 15–24): in the days to come, Israel will prosper, at the expense of Moab and Edom. The sceptre mentioned in verse 17 (the word can mean 'rod, staff, club, sceptre', but also 'tribe') is sometimes (for example, by the 11th-century Rabbi Ibn Ezra) taken to be a reference to David, who was victorious over these peoples (2 Samuel 8:2, 13–14).

Amalek is singled out for destruction (v. 20). The Kenites (v. 21) were assimilated into Israel (compare Judges 4:17ff). Asshur signifies the Assyrian empire (Mesopotamia). They did not become a lethal threat to Israel until much later, in the 8th century. Samaria, the capi-tal of the northern kingdom, was destroyed by them in 721BC, but there was an empire over many centuries and it may be that verse 22 refers to events unknown to us. Kittim is usually taken to mean Cyprus, and Eber is connected with Genesis 10:21–25, whose descendants included Abraham and many others (that is, people who did not receive God's promise). The detailed meaning is uncertain.

Orthodox Jews have regarded verse 17 as predicting the coming of 'the Messiah, whose advent will be like a star appearing in the heaven, and he will gather the dispersed of Israel' (so Nachmanides, c. 1194). However, 'modern Jews have found it increasingly difficult to believe in a miraculous divine intervention which will change the course of human history... doctrines connected with the coming of the Messiah... have seemed totally implausible' (Dan Cohn-Sherbok, *The Jewish Messiah*, SCM Press, 1997, p. 171).

FOR MEDITATION

Rabbi Cohn-Sherbok says, 'Rather than await the coming of a divinely-appointed deliverer... Jews should themselves strive to create a better world for all peoples.' To what extent do or should Christians agree with this?

TWO BIRDS *with* ONE SPEAR

'Convert from Islam to Christianity killed by her own family.' News items similar to this occur today in missionary prayer letters. We probably feel angry or sick at the thought of it. Yet today's chapter seems to present the same scenario. The similarities are disturbing and should not be waved aside lightly but, to understand them, we need first to consider this chapter in its own context.

Yoked to Baal-Peor

The people of Israel had settled temporarily in Shittim. They obviously had some contact with local Canaanites, who invited them to their sacrifices, and some of the people 'yoked' or 'joined themselves' to the gods of the Canaanites, particularly the Baal (that is, 'Lord') of Peor. Baal was often linked to a particular place, and there seems to be an oscillation between speaking of 'Baal' in the singular and 'baals' in the plural. The terminology (though not the concept) is similar to 'Our Lady of Lourdes/Walsingham' and so on. The Hebrew for 'yoke oneself' (vv. 3, 5) is rare in the Old Testament and we must work out its exact meaning as best we can from the context. It seems to imply more than attending a religious function out of politeness or respect, but rather adopting the worship of these other gods.

Exactly what these sacrifices were like, we don't know, but we do have evidence of all sorts of unholy Canaanite practices, such as 'sacred prostitution' with women, and sometimes men, attached to the shrine, and sacrificing children to the god Milcom (given as 'Molech' in the Old Testament, a distortion of the name to make it rhyme with the Hebrew word for 'shame'). The nearest equivalent today might be an orgy or drugs party. I imagine that Moses felt something like parents who see their teenagers going seriously off the rails. Such parents do not usually order their children to be 'impaled in the sun' (v. 4), and this initiative comes not from Moses but the Lord. So the leaders, those with the heaviest responsibility for the apostasy, are impaled and Moses orders the judges of the people to kill any who have joined themselves to Baal.

Zeal in action

At this point, when the people generally have apparently repented and are weeping over their sin and/or its punishment, Zimri waltzes in through the camp and into his tent with a Midianite woman named Cozbi. Both of them were people of high status, a Simeonite prince and the daughter of a chief of some sort. Derek Kidner writes, 'Zimri was no mere youth caught in an unguarded moment, but a man of standing, who flaunted his trophy before the whole penitent congregation.' Phinehas the priest is incensed at this and follows the couple into the tent. They are obviously close together (whether vertically or horizontally, we are not told), close enough for one spear to pierce and kill both of them. Then comes a surprise: the plague that we have not been told about is stopped. So, taking the narrative as it comes to us, we have to imagine a plague starting earlier—possibly the cause for Moses' seeking direction from God, and certainly a reason for weeping. So the plague is halted, although 24,000 (perhaps 24 companies: see comment on Numbers 1, pp. 108–109) have already died.

Phinehas and his descendants are granted a 'covenant of peace'— that is, God's promise that they will always be priests. This is similar to the covenant with David (2 Samuel 7; Psalms 89:3–4, 20–37; 132:11–18) that one of his descendants would always sit on the throne of Israel. As we know, there was no Israelite king for most of the period from the fall of Jerusalem in 587BC to the birth of Jesus. The Herods were of Edomite origin, appointed by the Romans, and certainly not recognized by the people of Judah. We have to reckon, then, with a conditional promise. Nevertheless, God's intention remained constant and, Christians believe, was confirmed for ever when Christ rose from the dead. We do not hear much about Phinehas in later times (that is, after Joshua 22:30–34), except that his name appears in genealogies (Ezra 7:5; 8:2; 1 Chronicles 6:4, 50; 9:20). Jesus himself provides a stark contrast to Phinehas: though innocent of all wrongdoing, he allowed himself to be pierced with a spear for our sake: 'They will look on the one whom they have pierced' (John 19:34, 37).

PRAYER

*Lord, when you looked upon the Israelites joining themselves
to other gods, what did you really want to do? When you look upon
the world today, its violence and hatred, and its lies, what do you
really want to do? Lord, show me how I can understand
your ways better, and move closer to the centre of your will.
Through Jesus Christ my Saviour. Amen.*

Another AUTHORIZED CENSUS

This chapter is not likely to fire the imagination of most readers, but there may be those who like accounts sheets, so here is a comparison with the numbers obtained from the census in Numbers 1.

Numbers: decline and growth

Tribe	Reuben	Simeon	Gad	Judah	Issachar	Zebulun
Num. 1	46,500	59,300	45,650	74,600	54,400	57,400
Num. 26	43,730	22,200	40,500	76,500	64,300	60,500
Increase/ decrease	-2,770	-37,100	-5,150	+1,900	+9,900	+3,100

Tribe	Ephraim	Manasseh	Benjamin	Dan	Asher	Naphtali
Num. 1	40,500	32,200	35,400	62,700	41,500	53,400
Num. 26	32,500	52,700	45,600	64,400	53,400	45,400
Increase/ decrease	-8,000	+20,500	+10,200	+1,700	+11,900	-8,000

The total 601,730 (or 601 'groups'?) is only slightly less than the 603,550 (or 603 'groups'?) who started out in Numbers 1. God has replaced those who died in the desert. He has no need to maintain numbers at any cost. The really big gain is Manasseh (no reason known —did some transfer to the other Joseph tribe somehow? Perhaps they fancied settling in Transjordan). The even bigger *loss* is in Simeon, possibly from being involved with the rebellion of Dathan and Abiram (ch. 16) and the Baal-Peor issue (25:14), possibly from a localized disease that is not mentioned, or some other reason. We do know that Simeon ceased to exist as an independent tribe early in Israel's history and became absorbed into Judah. This also means that talk about the 'twelve tribes' divided into groups of two (Judah and Benjamin) plus ten (the others, Joseph divided into Ephraim and Manasseh, with Levi left out of account) needs to be taken symbolically rather than completely literally. Nevertheless, the disciples of Jesus felt that they had to have a literal twelve and appointed Matthias when Judas left them (Acts 1:26).

Numbers and personal notes

The purpose of the census seems to be for military purposes, as in Numbers 1, but more importantly for the purpose of allocating land according to the size of the tribe (vv. 52–56). The method of distribution—by lot, with the assumption that the Lord would guide the result—has been almost entirely dropped, but I wonder if it would not give just as good results with less upset in certain situations!

The figures are interspersed with comments referring to incidents that are included in the earlier narrative, such as the stories of Nadab and Abihu (Leviticus 10) and Er and Onan, who 'spilled his seed' in order not to provide children for his dead brother (Genesis 38:6–10). The most remarkable is the note that Korah and company were swallowed up and became a warning (supporting the suggestion that these events are out of the ordinary and not the way that God works all the time) and that 'the sons of Korah did not die' (vv. 10–11). Jeremiah and Ezekiel, at a much later time in Israel's history, make the point that each one should die for his own sins and not for those of his father, and the reference to Korah's sons seems to be an early witness to this concern.

We shall come across the daughters of Zelophehad in chapters 27 and 36, but we note that they are included here in the official genealogical lists of Israel (v. 33). Other than that, it is difficult to see any useful applications of these chapters for 'the general reader'. They do give valuable information for research into forms of names, and if you are looking for an unusual name for a child (usually a son) you might get some inspiration—for example, how about Shephupham (v. 39)?

Looking over the whole chapter, Gordon Wenham comments:

> Despite these great setbacks, the total population of Israel after years of wandering is almost the same as it was at Sinai... and the people are on the verge of entering the promised land. In this way this table of census returns develops one of the great themes of the book of Numbers: God's promises to the patriarchs may be delayed by human sin but they are not ultimately frustrated by it (compare Romans 11). (Numbers, p. 190)

FOR REFLECTION

Wanted: People motivated by love, willing to commit suicide,
if necessary, by carrying the explosive gospel of peace
into enemy territory.

ZELOPHEHAD'S DAUGHTERS

Zelophehad had five daughters who were obviously a feisty bunch. They come to Moses with the question, 'Is it right that our father's inheritance should be lost simply because he had no sons? Should it not come to us, who are just as much his offspring as if we were male?' Moses has not faced this question before, but he doesn't bluster and improvise an answer—'This is quite irregular, not according to our tradition'. *He takes it to the Lord.* The ruling is given that the daughters are right and should be given inheritance among the tribes of Israel.

Human reasoning and God's guidance

The daughters give some unexpected information. First, their father was not a member of Korah's company who perished in the desert. The relevance seems to be that people who rebelled against God were executed and lost the right to their land. This would explain Jezebel's false accusations against Naboth in order to get him killed and his land made available for annexation by the king (1 Kings 21:5–10). However, they add that *he died for his own sin.* This might simply mean that he died early and they assume that he must have sinned. Or it may imply that he belonged to the generation who refused to believe God's promises and shared the scepticism of the ten spies who brought back a bad report of the promised land. If this is right, then Calvin has a good point to make: the daughters were asserting their faith in God's promises, that the land *would* be taken and they would have the possibility of an inheritance. They thus neatly dissociate themselves from their father's unbelief.

We note that this incident gives us some insight into ways in which God guides. The law is not simply given in one block, dropped down from heaven by God without any human content. It arises because people realize that they need to know what to do in a new situation. They are expected to use their common sense (hence the reasoning of Zelophehad's daughters) and to seek God's guidance. We don't have Moses' advantage, who 'spoke with God face to face' (12:8), but we do have a vast amount of extra knowledge from all sorts of different disciplines. We have the New Testament, and we have the Holy Spirit and church tradition. We have seen previous incidents brought to God for a decision, which became a precedent and part of the case law of

Israel—for example, in Leviticus 24:10–23 (the Egyptian-Israelite blasphemer); Numbers 9:6–8 (those unclean and unable to keep the Passover); and 15:32–36 (the man gathering sticks on the sabbath).

Joshua takes over

In the second half of the chapter, Moses passes on the leadership role to Joshua. Two contrasting points are made. First, Joshua is the true successor to Moses. Moses lays his hand upon him, recalling similar actions where this gesture indicates a transfer—sin transferred to a goat (Leviticus 16) or to other sacrifices (Leviticus 1:4; 4:4) and the guilt of hearing blasphemy transferred to the blasphemer (Leviticus 24:13). 'The laying on of hands' is found as an established practice in the New Testament as a means of commissioning leaders—Stephen and the other deacons (Acts 6:6), Saul and Barnabas (Acts 13:3), and Timothy (1 Timothy 4:14). Joshua's succession is confirmed by the miraculous crossing of the Jordan (Joshua 3:14–17), paralleling the crossing of the Red Sea under Moses (Exodus 14), and the vision of the commander of the Lord's army on 'holy ground' before the conquest (Joshua 5:13–15), paralleling Moses' burning bush incident (Exodus 3). It seems natural and in line with these examples that many churches today use the laying on of hands as a visible sign of passing on authority that both encourages the faith of the one prayed for and the congregation, and is a sign of the commitment of those praying to ask in faith and to expect to see answers.

On the other hand, though, Moses gives Joshua only *some* of his authority (v. 20). Joshua will not be exactly like Moses. He will not speak with God face to face but will rely on Eleazar the priest and the Urim and Thummim method to discern the Lord's will (v. 21). An era has passed and the people will have to face up to the difficult fact that things are not what they used to be. The strength and definiteness of God's guidance varies from period to period. Even today we have to learn to develop the enormously difficult skill of sensitivity to the leading of God's Spirit.

FOR REFLECTION

Does your church practise the laying on of hands, for confirmations by the bishop, for prayer for healing, for commissioning? How vulnerable are you when you participate in this and how open to receiving visible answers?

OFFERINGS *through the* YEAR

These chapters outline the regular offerings—daily, weekly, monthly and annual.

The daily offerings

Whatever other feasts might be taking place, two lambs were to be offered every day, together with the usual cereal and drink offerings. These are called 'offerings by fire' and 'continual', but 28:10 implies that they are burnt offerings. They are intended as a permanent reminder that God is ever-present and not to be taken for granted, a holy God in the midst of a sinful people, but a loving God who has chosen the people, who has made a way for them to approach him, and who forgives sin. The burnt offerings have to be offered every day whether there is any evident public wrongdoing or not, for the difference between God and human beings is always there.

On the sabbath day, these sacrifices, whole burnt offerings, are doubled. Whether the extras were to be offered morning and evening or both at one time, we are not told. The sabbath was a holy day and the extra sacrifices gave visible expression to that fact. At the beginning of *each* month (v. 11, compare v. 14) there is a 2-1-7-1 combination—two bullocks, one ram and seven lambs (plus the usual cereal and drink offerings) as a burnt offering and also (v. 15) one he-goat for a sin offering.

Less frequent offerings

We then move on to the annual Passover on the fourteenth day of the first month, to be followed by a seven-day festival. On the first and last days of the festival, work was forbidden, and unleavened bread was eaten throughout this period. Jewish people today scrupulously clear out the old leaven thoroughly before Passover (*Pesach*), after which they introduce new leaven into their diet again. It is a reminder of the need to remove anything impure from our lives, and both Jesus and Paul refer to it in this way (Mark 8:15; 1 Corinthians 5:6–8; Galatians 5:9; see comment on Leviticus 2:11, pp. 32–33).

At Passover, sacrifices were offered as on the first day of the month (the 2-1-7-1 pattern). Presumably there would be extras on the sabbath day, wherever that occurred during the week. It is to be hoped that the priests had an efficient person to manage the diary!

On the day of first fruits, that is, when new grain was offered, they were to offer (yes, you've guessed it) 2-1-7-1 (vv. 26–30).

Chapter 29 moves on to the seventh month. The festival of trumpets was celebrated on the first day (a 1-1-7-1 formula this time, vv. 3, 5). No work was to be done—except for the trumpeters and the sacrificing priests, of course. Then came another 1-1-7-1 on the tenth day, and a seven-day event from the fifteenth onwards. For mathematicians and accountants, the sequence of sacrifices for these seven days goes: 13-2-14-1; 12-2-14-1; and on down to 7-2-14-1 on the last day (vv. 32–34). Finally, on the eighth day there is a return to the 1-1-7-1 pattern, and work is forbidden.

Offerings of joy

From all this, we might get the impression that Israelite religion was a big effort and a burden. After all, these sacrifices were whole burnt offerings and no human being ate any of them. However, there is a clue in 29:39 that this is not how we should picture it: '…in addition to your votive offerings and your freewill offerings… and your offerings of well-being (peace offerings)' (see comment on Leviticus 3 and Leviticus 7, pp. 34–35, 44–47). The atmosphere would have resembled that of a joyful feast. However, the number of sacrifices required is considerable and there must have been times when it seemed very hard to see these animals simply going up in smoke. We cannot imagine God being pleased with these sacrifices for their own sake. The prophets remind us forcefully that if we do not take care of the poor and needy, God does not want our sacrifices. 1 John 4:20 echoes this: 'Those who say, "I love God," and hate their brothers or sisters, are liars; for those who do not love a brother or sister whom they have seen, cannot love God whom they have not seen.'

FOR FURTHER REFLECTION

'Then you may turn [your tithe] into money. With the money secure in hand, go to the place that the Lord your God will choose; spend the money for whatever you wish—oxen, sheep, wine, strong drink, or whatever you desire. And you shall eat there in the presence of the Lord your God, you and your household rejoicing together.'

Deuteronomy 14:25–26

Vows: Binding *or* Not?

The basic rationale of this section is clear: if you make a vow, and you are free to make it, the vow stands and you must not break it. If you are under the authority of another person, father or husband, then he has the authority to annul the vow *at the time he hears of it*. It is clear that this legislation does not meet today's equality assumptions, for it is only women who are regarded as under someone else's authority—father's before marriage and husband's after marriage. Widows and divorced women are able to speak for themselves.

Free to make vows?

The relevance of this idea for today is not entirely agreed. There are many Christian denominations or groups where women are supposed to be under their husband's authority—and many where they are not. The requirement cannot really be traced back to this chapter, since Old Testament laws were given for a particular society and social context. However, certain New Testament references seem to support the view, especially 1 Timothy 2:8–15, which has occasioned an enormous amount of discussion, both scholarly and popular. Perhaps all we can do at this point is to insist that those who take delight in Ephesians 5:22 should note carefully 5:21 and 25.

Certain cases not covered specifically by this legislation on vows would probably have been dealt with quite easily by following the principles laid down. For example, a male youth still under his father's authority would presumably also need parental approval for making a binding vow, and probably a widow taken by her brotherin-law in order to 'raise up children' for the deceased man would be considered as married. But what of those who are not intelligent enough to know what they are doing in making a vow? Or those who make vows that are simply impossible to keep, or that conflict with a moral law?

Rash, foolish and sinful vows

There are some examples in the Old Testament of vows broken, apparently with God's approval. While on the run from Saul, David comes across a rich farmer called Nabal (meaning 'Fool'!). David's band of soldiers could simply take what they want by force, but instead they ask Nabal to give them some supplies. He is abusive and refuses to give anything, at which point David makes a vow: 'God do so to David and more also, if by morning I leave so much as one male of all who belong to him.' (Yes, David was a rough soldier and this narrative does not lend itself to 'Be-like-David' sermons.) David is persuaded to change his mind by Abigail, Nabal's wife, who sends a substantial present to David and asks for forgiveness for the folly of her husband. David responds, 'Blessed be the Lord… who sent you to meet me today! Blessed be your good sense… you have kept me today from bloodguilt' (1 Samuel 25:11–35). This passage is instructive since it suggests that a change of circumstances would give a logical reason for regarding a vow as void. As in the case of prophecy, tacitly assumed to be conditional, and other laws which *assume* but do not *express* exceptions, a vow is understood to be conditional. In David's case, the reason for vowing vengeance on Nabal was removed and the vow did not need to be carried through. Moreover, there is a hint that David's vow was not only completely over the top, but actually sinful ('bloodguilt'), and for that reason might be repented of. See also 1 Samuel 14:24–30, 43–45 and comment on Numbers 6 (pp. 118–119).

A lady I once knew made a vow when she was ill: 'If I recover, I will attend the 8 am Holy Communion service every week.' It wasn't always sensible for her to venture out and walk the mile and a half to church, especially on icy mornings, but she felt a sense of compulsion. Yet it was quite difficult to suggest that she might break the vow.

The main concerns evident in the Old Testament seem to be that vows should not be undertaken lightly or unadvisedly and that setting them aside is a serious matter. But they are not absolutely and utterly binding in all circumstances. Vows are not the only situation in which we might be forced to compromise.

FOR REFLECTION

What sort of practical help might be given to those trapped by a foolish vow? Would some sort of substitute vow fit some circumstances? How can people be helped to know in their hearts about God's grace and forgiveness?

DEALING *with the* MIDIANITES

Here we read about the last battle before Moses dies and the book of Numbers ends. It gives us a chance to look back over a whole range of horrifying events and ask what we make of them.

Review of the story so far

After the conquest of Canaan, there will be no more warfare in which everything is 'put to the ban' or 'devoted to destruction', except for isolated incidents (the Amalekites in 1 Samuel 15). We have witnessed rebellions and judgment—either directly by God (Taberah, then quails with plague, 11:1–3, 31–34; plague after disbelieving Joshua and Caleb, 14:36–38; Korah, Dathan and Abiram, 16:31–35, 46–50) or at his command (gathering sticks on the sabbath, 15:32–36) or because he allowed the people to be defeated (ch. 14). We have seen the death penalty applied for transgressions of the law (Leviticus 10, strange fire; Leviticus 24, blaspheming the name of God). We have seen Miriam and Aaron, and even Moses, under judgment (ch. 12; 20:12, 24–29; 27:12–14). We have seen the annihilation of whole groups of people by God's command (Hormah, Sihon and Og, and now Midian, 21:1–3, 23–26, 33–35).

We have come across the *lex talionis*, 'an eye for an eye and a tooth for a tooth' (Leviticus 24:17–21). For reasons that I don't understand, God's policy in revelation seems to be very low key and a matter of moving people from where they are to where they should be. We know that Jesus indicated that the Old Testament law did not go far enough: love your friends, yes, but love your enemies also (Matthew 5:43–46). The *lex talionis* may have served to limit venge-ance but it was not good enough. Death for adultery? 'Let the one who is without sin throw the first stone.'

Lessons from horrific events

The Midianites were apparently a large 'confederation of tribes, associated with smaller groups, such as… the Moabites' (Wenham). The battle in chapter 31 seems to involve this particular group 'on the plains of Moab' (v. 12). The numbers of people and animals captured seems impossibly high (including 675,000 sheep and 32,000 virgins).

The basic storyline is that the Israelites take only a limited number of warriors, representing the whole people of Israel, that is, 1000 (if correct) from each tribe. They defeat the Midianites without losing a single soldier, which speaks to them and to future generations of the Lord's special protection in this battle, and of being in line with his will. They kill all the males (the context implies adult males, v. 7) but bring the women back to the camp to Moses. He is angry and asks if they have failed to realize that it was the women who led Israel into sin.

Some commentators suggest that there may have been religious prostitutes involved who enticed the Israelite men to worship Baal-Peor. Even though that is quite likely, for Canaanite religion did make use of cult prostitutes, most of the women could not have been involved in this way. The implication is that women as well as men have responsibility for their actions.

The rules of engagement for this type of 'holy war' required that all people, men and women, young and old (Joshua 6:21), must be put to death. In this particular case, the male children are killed, but the 'children among the women' (v. 18), that is, the young girls who have not had sexual intercourse, are allowed to live. Thus the Israelites take steps to avoid the raising of a Midianite Moses! The abused adopt the practices of their abusers, though the Israelites had more justification than the Egyptians did. Looking back on these customs, we cannot as Christians condone them, but we are reminded that there may be wrong attitudes that we absorb from our surrounding culture that still need identification, repentance and change.

What is clear from the whole narrative of Leviticus and Numbers, whether we think these events happened or not, is that God is holy and that sin against him is much more serious than we are apt to think. We cannot presume that 'God is love' (according to our own ideas of love) and that any approach to him is bound to succeed. If we have failed to catch something of the sense of the awesome nature of God, we have missed the most important message of this part of the Old Testament—and we will find no support for our view in the New Testament.

FOR REFLECTION

The temptation to remove one's enemies once and for all is very
enticing to those who are convinced that God's ways are their ways.
how should those act who 'have the mind of Christ'?
(1 Corinthians 2:16).

A GOOD IDEA *of* REUBEN & GAD

Today's chapter gives us a good example of how negotiations ought to be conducted. The tribes of Reuben and Gad (half of Manasseh suddenly appear in verse 33) see that the land east of the Jordan, where they have been living and fighting, is good for cattle, so they ask Moses if they can settle there. Moses is at first affronted, assuming that they intend simply to settle down and let the others go over the Jordan on their own. This will be bad for morale (v. 7), just as the ten spies' report was. It will lay the whole people open to God's judgment once more if they draw back from entering into the promises made to their ancestors. It will spoil the unity of the twelve tribes, who have been acting together and, in fact, took the land east of the Jordan by concerted effort.

Satisfactory negotiation

The petitioners seem to have gone away to think about this, for in verse 16 we are told that they 'came up to him' and promised to help the main body of Israel conquer the land west of the Jordan before returning to the east to settle. They will build sheepfolds and towns and leave their animals, wives and children on the eastern side. (They did not have to start from scratch but rebuilt various towns, according to verses 34, 37—and the towns envisaged would have been rather basic.) We presume that most of the other families accompanied their husbands/fathers over the Jordan (Joshua 4:1). To leave families behind, even in well-defended cities, would demand considerable faith in God's power to protect. This is true of many situations in the world today. Where Christians live in the midst of hostile or unsympathetic neighbours and/or under antagonistic regimes, security is not merely a matter of smoke alarms and Chubb locks, but of life and death. In these places, trust in God is no optional extra for the frills of life, but a desperate necessity.

Moses agrees to their request but not without giving them a severe warning that they must keep their promise. Although described as the meekest man on earth (12:3), Moses could be quite sharp. Humility does not require letting people get away with it. The famous expression, 'Be sure your sin will find you out' occurs in this context

(v. 23). The Israelites had seen many examples of God's judgment but Moses does not specify what sort of payback to expect. It would be 'sin against the Lord' and consequences cannot be avoided.

Thinking openly before God

It is noteworthy that in Moses' exhortation to Gad and Reuben in verses 20–24, he uses the expression 'before the Lord' four times, with regard to taking up arms, crossing the Jordan, subduing the land and taking possession. There are extra references to being 'free of obligation to the Lord' (that is, with regard to further participation west of the Jordan) and 'sinning against the Lord'. Plainly the whole operation is carried out in the conviction and consciousness that God is right there in the midst. This realization can produce opposite reactions: 'Woe is me, for I am a man of unclean lips and I live among a people of unclean lips' and 'Go away from me, Lord, for I am a sinful man' (Isaiah 6:5; Luke 5:8); or 'If God be for us, who can be against us' (Romans 8:31). Both these aspects—immediate chastening and long-term blessing—are expressed in the name 'Immanuel' (Isaiah 7:14; contrast 8:8 with 8:10).

Some commentators have assumed that Reuben and Gad were guilty of a worldly attitude in going after material benefits (as did Lot, Genesis 13:10–11, who ended up in Sodom). Calvin may be nearer the mark: the enlargement of Israelite territory is an example of God's bringing good out of human sin. The term 'Canaan' refers to the land west of the Jordan, so the land on the east was not part of the original promise. Both suggestions, however, seem unfair since Israel had always been promised a land flowing with milk and honey, a material blessing. Rather, Reuben and Gad give us an example of thoughtlessness which was corrected by their being open to listen to Moses' rebuke.

FOR PRAYER AND REFLECTION

Lord, please give me good ideas, and make me ready to recognize that they might be improved, to submit them to others, and to surrender the copyright, that together we may discover your perfect will.

From EGYPT *to the* PLAINS *of* MOAB

There aren't many people who will relish reading this chapter—or writing a commentary on it. (It reminds me of a old railway timetable from the heyday of steam.) But it does contain some important information and reminders. First of all, Moses is commanded by the Lord to keep a careful record of the places at which they have stopped as they journeyed towards the land of Canaan. Scholars have sometimes questioned whether written records could have been kept at this early stage of Israel's history, though there are other allusions in Exodus 17:7; 24:4–8; 34:27 and in Deuteronomy. The number of stopping stations is forty (42 if you count the start at Rameses and the end at the Plains of Moab) and this *may* be significant—but there seems to be no way of deciding exactly what the significance is. There are difficult problems in working out the exact route taken by the Israelites. See the map on page 27 for the traditional suggestion.

Remember—accurately

It is important for the nation to *remember* what happened and how the Lord led, provided for, corrected, taught and delivered them, finally bringing them to the promised land itself. Those who have kept a diary or, better, a journal, will probably confirm that it is vitally important as a memory jogger and a corrective to both rose-tinted spectacles and unhelpfully dark glasses. On the one hand, we can forget unpleasant incidents, times when we have made mistakes or have done wrong, and we can begin to look back to the 'good old days' (see 11:5, 'We remember the fish in Egypt'—but they forgot the slavery). On the other hand, we can forget times when God intervened in our lives and led us bit by bit through many difficulties.

Looking back over a period of time can help us to see God's hand at work, when it may not have been obvious at the time. God does not command us to keep a diary, but it is a good idea and one of the learning points from this Old Testament passage. He certainly does command us to remember what he has done for us, and the book of Deuteronomy is particularly keen to exhort the people to *remember and not to forget* certain key facts—their condition in Egypt and how the Lord delivered them and led them. Various aids were prescribed to help them—the piles of stones along the way, the blue tassels on their garments (15:37–40), and the brief 'creed' that was to be recited every year when they brought the first fruits to the sanctuary (Deuteronomy 26:2–3, 5–10). This points towards the 'practice of the presence of God' recommended by Brother Lawrence (1605–91).

One God—the foundation for dialogue

Verse 4 reminds us that the judgments against Egypt were not just against the nation but against its gods (as stated in Exodus 12:12). A major concern and emphasis of the Old Testament from Exodus onwards is to establish the fact that Yahweh, the Lord, is the only God for Israel, and by implication the only true God who exists, 'for in six days the Lord made heaven and earth…' (Exodus 20:11). The question of whether people might worship the same God under a different name is legitimate. Compare Genesis 14:19, where Melchizedek refers to 'El Elyon (= God Most High), maker of heaven and earth'. In Genesis 14:22, Abraham simply adds 'Yahweh' in front of this description. 'El Elyon' is a name for a god that is found in texts from Canaan. This warns us against glib and simplistic assumptions when we enter into dialogue with people of other faiths. With Jews and Muslims, we work on the assumption that we all believe in one God, the only God who exists and who created the universe. It is more helpful to talk about the characteristics of God, rather than using the language of 'worshipping different gods' (at least one of which doesn't exist). It is surprising (to me, anyhow) just how liberating and instructive it can be to speak with people of other faiths about their convictions and ideas. God is surely at work through all the world.

FOR PRAYER AND MEDITATION

Lord, give me a clear apprehension and appreciation of your dealings with me in the past, that in the present and future I may live closer to you.

BOUNDARIES & LEVITICAL CITIES

Pretty boring stuff? Try to put yourself in the place of an ancient Israelite, part of an huge crowd who have been wandering around the desert like refugees for forty years. No one in the crowd has known any other life—except Joshua and Caleb. And now the leader actually tells you the places that you are going to conquer: you will take possession of the land that you can see over the Jordan, stretching all the way to the great sea (that we know as the Mediterranean).

Of course, it's not possible to know exactly what the people felt. The situation of most readers of this commentary is totally different: towns are much larger generally—and in towns without walls, attitudes and mindset are quite different. We are not used to thinking of fighting for land, without which we can never become a nation. We don't—on the whole—have the same cause for resentment at the treatment we've received from the people we will now have to attack. Still, we know *something* of the feeling of dreams becoming reality and the difference between dreaming and achieving. The Israelites have now come to the brink of realizing their dream, a dream based on God's promise to their ancestors hundreds of years before, a dream that has faded from time to time and been boosted by encouragements and rebukes along the way.

A huge promised land

The bulk of chapter 34 deals with the boundaries of the promised land (see the map on page 26). The land allotted covers the area between the Mediterranean on the west and the Jordan on the east, with a fair bit of territory east of the Jordan in the north. To gain this land, the Israelites would wage war for many years—and they would not be totally successful. Tyre, Sidon and Byblos never became part of Israel's territory. Canaan is mentioned as a geographical entity in Egyptian texts from the 15th century BC onwards and generally corresponds to the area indicated in 34:1–12 (that is, not including the land east of the Jordan). The earliest reference to 'Israel' in a source outside the Bible comes from the Pharaoh Merneptah (or Marniptah, or similar) in about 1220BC, who claims that 'Israel is no more', presumably because he has defeated and wiped it out. Well, we all make mistakes.

Tribal boundaries

Having delineated the outer boundaries of the whole of Israel, Moses goes on to specify the men from each tribe who will 'apportion the land' (by lot), under the overall supervision of Eleazar the priest and Joshua (34:17). Of the ten other leaders mentioned, only Caleb has appeared previously.

In chapter 35, we move on to deal with the Levites. They are allotted 48 towns or cities, including the 'cities of refuge' (see the next reading). In this way they are distributed throughout the nation and should have acted as 'Levite leaven', people dedicated to preserving and passing on Israel's traditions, especially with respect to sacrifices and the Law. The Levites needed some safe place where they could live *by right*, and they are given some pasture land around each of their allotted cities. It has been estimated that this would not have been sufficient to supply their needs without the supplement that came through sacrifices offered. A cubit was about 46cm, so the pasture land measures 1000m square, with the town in the middle. It is likely that, at first, the towns were quite small and took up a very small part of the allotted land. As time went on, it seems likely that the edge of the pasture land would have been extended correspondingly.

The means of provision tallies with the idea of physical security (with hard work) plus trust in God. Those dedicated to making God's word known often find that their honesty and loving care are appreciated, and people support them willingly. However, there are times when many people face poverty, or when a hard message has to be delivered and freewill offerings are sparse. Priestly deviousness may make for short-term profit, but will lead ultimately to disaster. Either the people refuse to support them or God brings judgment, as was the case with Eli's sons (1 Samuel 2:27–34; 4:17). In the Old Testament itself, Israel sins and loses its land and its right to the land. It is therefore impossible to establish from this text that modern Israel should seek these original borders. But the Lord still definitely requires of all of us 'to do justice, and to love kindness, and to walk humbly with him' (Micah 6:8).

FOR REFLECTION

Have I any dreams that were once real and have faded? What reassessment is called for, and what positive plans under God?

CITIES *of* REFUGE

It's difficult to imagine God's devising this scheme of cities of refuge
—prejudiced in favour of good runners—from scratch. Nevertheless,
there is a great deal in this practice that teaches vitally important principles concerning life and death. The basic ruling is that if someone
kills a person accidentally, he is allowed to make for the nearest city
of refuge and be safe from the 'avenger of blood', that is, the kinsman
of the deceased who has the responsibility of avenging the death.
Presumably the same rules applied to women, though they would
rarely apply. The case of Jael would have come under the rules of war
(despite her terrible violation of expected hospitality), as (obviously)
would the woman who dropped a millstone on Abimelech's head
outside the city wall (Judges 9:53).

Benefits and anomalies

The practical value of the system was that it provided a procedure
that people could agree to—laws too much ahead of their time
simply do not work, as we know. The seriousness of killing a person,
even accidentally, was acknowledged and the penalty was severe. The
manslaughterer had the opportunity to go hastily to a city of refuge,
present his case to 'the congregation' and be formally and legally
granted permission to live within the city as a refugee. We are not
told what scope there was for earning a living, or whether there was
any provision for city council support for long-term resident aliens.
Presumably relatives would have been able to visit freely.

We can easily imagine anomalies: if a one-legged man killed the
relative of a decathlon champion, what would be his chances of ever
reaching the city of refuge? If a man like Samson accidentally killed
someone, would the avenger of blood try very hard to catch up with
him? No doubt these problems were faced and solved by the elders
in more or less satisfactory ways, but the system remains imperfect
and we have to think in terms of a transitional arrangement that God
wanted to see improved upon.

David 'beat the system' at least twice: he committed adultery
(which attracted the death penalty) and virtual murder (killing in
battle) but Nathan told him, 'The Lord has put away your sin.' David

was also persuaded to take back his son Absalom and not put him to death, despite the fact that he had killed Amnon (2 Samuel 13:23–29; 14:21–24, 31–33). This could be regarded as a case of 'one law for the rich and one for the poor'—as it probably was. Nevertheless it is used to indicate the possibility that sins for which there was no sacrifice might, by God's grace, be forgiven.

Theological rationale

The key to the theological undergirding of the practice is given clearly in verse 33: 'no expiation can be made for the land, for the blood that is shed in it, except by the blood of the one who shed it'. The rule emphasizes in the strongest way the sacredness of human life. Whether the death is caused by a circumstance that could not be foreseen or because of negligence, the result is the same. Safeguards are put in place but they are not foolproof: a person cannot be convicted on the evidence of a single witness. But could circumstantial evidence be taken into account? The reliability of the witnesses is not commented upon, and we know that collusion was possible, as in the case of Naboth's vineyard (1 Kings 21:8–14), when he was falsely accused by 'two scoundrels' and stoned to death. Common sense is also required when administering law and it is to be assumed that elders were not easily hoodwinked.

The most surprising thing about the arrangements is that the refugee is allowed to return to his own place in safety when the high priest dies. No rationale is given but, in view of verse 33, mentioned above, we must presume that the high priest's death in some way atoned for the sin of bloodshed, and removed the pollution from the land. Christians cannot help seeing a parallel with the death of Jesus, our high priest, as a sacrifice for sin—a sacrifice such as was not provided for under the law.

FOR PRAYER AND REFLECTION

'Deliver me from bloodshed/bloodguiltiness, O God, O God
of my salvation, and my tongue will sing aloud of your saving
righteousness… For you have no delight in sacrifice; if I were to give
a burnt offering, you would not be pleased. The sacrifice acceptable
to God is a broken spirit; a broken and contrite heart, O God, you
will not despise. Do good to Zion in your good pleasure; rebuild the
walls of Jerusalem, then you will delight in right sacrifices.'

Psalm 51:14, 16–19

GREATER LOVE HATH NO WOMAN...

A ticklish problem is foreseen: it has been agreed that Zelophehad's daughters should inherit their father's land, but if they marry a man belonging to another tribe, ownership of the land will pass out of the tribe of Manasseh. Moses accepts the logic of the argument (v. 5) and gives them the Lord's command (we presume that he sought guidance before pronouncing, or else just knew the answer, v. 6). They are to marry good Manassite boys. Choice of marriage partners was already restricted to within the people of Israel—and people like Ruth who joined themselves to Israel—so now it is restricted further. Western readers unfamiliar with the system of arranged marriages will probably react to this more strongly than Zelophehad's daughters did. We are not told of any misgivings or heartache, simply that they 'did as the Lord had commanded Moses' (v. 10). We have hints in other parts of the Old Testament concerning the procedures adopted for finding a suitable wife: Abraham sent his trusty servant back to his own people to find a girl, who turned out to be Rebekah (Genesis 24). Jacob would possibly have done better to have a skilled and experienced negotiator working for him when he made a bid for Rachel. He worked for seven years for her and got Leah, an unwanted, preconditional bonus, as well as the obligation to work for Laban for another seven years (Genesis 29:15–30). Is this an argument against love marriages—or against naïvety, or dishonesty? At least the rivalry and unhappiness that Jacob's marriages set up led to the birth of twelve sons—possibly an example of how God brings good from evil?

Tribal identities still lost

The tribes did not all, in fact, maintain their identities. Simeon seems to have been absorbed into Judah at an early stage. The ten northern tribes were defeated in 721BC by the Assyrians, who exiled many thousands of Israelites and brought in similar numbers of foreigners from outside, thus destroying national identity. Judah survived and Benjamin was linked with it (Paul was from the tribe of Benjamin, Philippians 3:5), but we refer to 'Judah' and 'Jews' rather than the southern tribes of Judah and Benjamin—plus, of course, Levi.

It is assumed here that tribal identity is a good thing and must be preserved. But bearing in mind what we have seen about the transitional nature of many Old Testament laws (they do not represent God's ideal or final word on a particular situation), we should ask whether it is necessarily good and what it says to us today.

Anything good about tribalism?

We know something of the evils of nationalism and tribalism (for example, in Ireland, the Balkans and Rwanda) but what were the good features of the tribal system in Israel? The main one seems to come from the need to *remember*, as is commanded many times in the Old Testament, particularly in the book of Deuteronomy (see 5:15; 7:18; 32:7). The people of Israel are to remember how they got there—by the grace of God who performed mighty acts on their behalf. Because of that, they are to seek to please him in all that they do. They are to learn from past mistakes and past blessings. Their sense of being a people brought into existence by God, not through their own intrinsic goodness but through his choosing to set his love upon them, will help them to live to please him. The fact that they were slaves in the land of Egypt will help them to remember to treat their own slaves and the vulnerable among them with respect and care. The sins that their ancestors were guilty of, and God's judgment upon them, will help to give them a healthy awe and reverence towards God. Some of these considerations also translate into carrying the tribe's history—or the family's history.

But is it any loss to people living in Britain today that no one carries with them the memory of the history of the Angles, Saxons, Danes and Normans who invaded and settled many centuries ago? How important is it to maintain a separate Welsh or Scottish identity? Rahab, Ruth, and others became part of the history of Israel. Perhaps this is the significant thing about those who settle in any new country—to accept and be accepted, to identify with what is good in the new culture and to become part of it. Zelophehad's daughters give us many more questions than they can answer.

FOR REFLECTION

Looking back over the storyline in Leviticus and Numbers,
what are the overall lessons that emerge? To what extent do
they translate into lessons for our own past and present?
What important continuities would you like to be preserved
from your own past, going into the future?

NOTES

NOTES

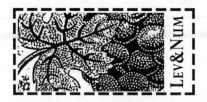

LEV&NUM

THE PEOPLE'S BIBLE COMMENTARY

VOUCHER SCHEME

The People's Bible Commentary (PBC) provides a range of readable, accessible commentaries that will grow into a library covering the whole Bible.

To help you build your PBC library, we have a voucher scheme that works as follows: a voucher is printed on this page of each People's Bible Commentary volume (as above). These vouchers count towards free copies of other books in the series.

For every four purchases of PBC volumes you are entitled to a further volume FREE.

Please find the coupon for the PBC voucher scheme opposite.

All you need do:

- Cut out the vouchers from the PBCs you have purchased and attach them to the coupon.

- Complete your name and address details, and indicate your choice of free book from the list on page 192.

- Take the coupon to your local Christian bookshop who will exchange it for your free PBC book; or send the coupon straight to BRF who will send you your free book direct. Please allow 28 days for delivery.

Please note that PBC volumes provided under the voucher scheme are subject to availability. If your first choice is not available, you may be sent your second choice of book.

THE PEOPLE'S
BIBLE COMMENTARY

VOUCHER SCHEME COUPON

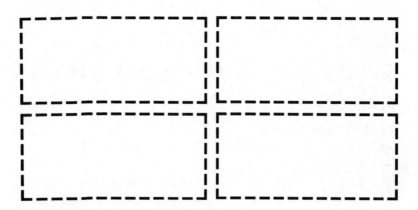

Customer and bookseller should both complete the form overleaf.

TO BE COMPLETED BY THE CUSTOMER

My choice of free PBC volume is:
(Please indicate a first and second choice;
all volumes are supplied subject to
availability.)

- ❏ Leviticus and Numbers
- ❏ Joshua and Judges
- ❏ 1 & 2 Samuel
- ❏ 1 & 2 Kings
- ❏ Chronicles to Nehemiah
- ❏ Job
- ❏ Psalms 1—72
- ❏ Psalms 73—150
- ❏ Proverbs
- ❏ Jeremiah
- ❏ Ezekiel
- ❏ Nahum to Malachi
- ❏ Matthew
- ❏ Mark
- ❏ Luke
- ❏ John
- ❏ Romans
- ❏ 1 Corinthians
- ❏ 2 Corinthians
- ❏ Galatians and Thessalonians
- ❏ Ephesians to Colossians
  and Philemon
- ❏ Timothy, Titus and Hebrews
- ❏ James to Jude

Name: . . . .
Address: . . . .
. . . .
Postcode: . . . .

TO BE COMPLETED BY THE BOOKSELLER

(Please complete the following.
Coupons redeemed will be credited to
your account for the value of the
book(s) supplied as indicated above.
Please note that only coupons correctly
completed with original vouchers will
be accepted for credit.)

Name: . . . .
Address: . . . .
. . . .
Postcode: . . . .
Account Number: . . . .

Completed coupons should be
sent to: BRF, PBC Voucher
Scheme, First Floor, Elsfield Hall,
15–17 Elsfield Way, Oxford
OX2 8FG.

Tel 01865 319700; Fax 01865
319701; e-mail enquiries@brf.org.uk
Registered Charity No. 233280

**THIS OFFER IS AVAILABLE IN THE UK
ONLY**
**PLEASE NOTE: ALL VOUCHERS ATTACHED
TO THE COUPON MUST BE ORIGINAL
COPIES.**